· *A Dales Album* ·

· A DALES ALBUM ·

A Pictorial History of the Yorkshire Dales

MARIE HARTLEY AND JOAN INGILBY

J. M. Dent & Sons Ltd
London

First published 1991
Text © Marie Hartley and Joan Ingilby 1991

This book is set in $11/13\frac{1}{2}$ pt Old Style
Printed in Great Britain by
Butler & Tanner Ltd, Frome and London

J. M. Dent & Sons Ltd
91 Clapham High Street, London SW4 7TA

British Library Cataloguing in Publication Data for this title is available upon request

ISBN: 0 460 86023.2

· Contents ·

The Past lives on; the Future's still unseen
Christy

· *Preface and Acknowledgments* ·

A Dales Album covers the area of the Yorkshire Dales from Nidderdale on the south to the borders of Durham on the north, and it includes Dentdale and Garsdale, which were formerly in Yorkshire but are now in Cumbria.

By means of photographs *A Dales Album* attempts to give a pictorial history of the dales from prehistoric times to the present day. With this in mind we have specially taken many photographs; we have drawn on our archives for others which could not be taken now, and we have enlisted the help of friends and curators of museums who have lent us old and new photographs from their albums and collections. Inevitably there is an emphasis on the late Victorian period to the present day, and to modify this we have written introductions to the seven sections and have composed informative captions.

The story of the Yorkshire Dales divides roughly into stages: prehistory, the Dark Ages, the Middle Ages, the rise of the yeomen, the industrial era, economic decline, and finally tourism. It is one of constant flux over the centuries, with farming as the underlying constant.

Many of the photographs have to be representative. For example, it would take a very large book or several volumes to depict every prehistoric site, or every castle or abbey, or yeoman's house, or every family group (so often delightful) from old albums. We have therefore made a choice based on the theme of the book.

We wish to thank our friends Dr G. C. Farnell and Mrs M. Farnell for their enthusiastic support in finding suitable photographs and in enlarging and copying our own and borrowed ones. Their co-operation has been invaluable. We have enjoyed discussing the work with Mr and Mrs D. S. Hall, and we thank Mr J. Edenbrow, Mr and Mrs G. Ellison, Mr and Mrs F. Carr, Mr F. J. Willis and Mrs D. Lee, also the many people who have checked the captions which concern them. Rather than repeat many names we hope that those acknowledged in the following list will accept our thanks for their help, not forgetting the cups of tea so welcome in the hot summer of 1989.

The photographs are reproduced by courtesy of the following: Mrs A. Alderson, 61, 248; Mr C. Alderson, 120, 193; J. Allan Cash/The British Council/Corporation of Richmond/County Archivist, 82, 245; Canon E. Allen, 170; Miss M. Burrow, 184; Mrs A. E. Barthram, 161, 162, 226; Mr T. Bell, 112, 188; Mr J. Blythe, 62, 122, 210, 237; Mrs D. A. Bradley, 55, 87; Mr J. B. Brown, 102; Mr and Mrs F. Carr, 60, 84; Mr C. Chapman, 202; Mrs P. Clayton, 173; Craven Museum, Skipton, 149, 249; Mr G. Cross, 48, 203, 211; Mr J. Cowan, 179; Miss N. Cutcliffe Hyne, 174; the Dales Countryside Museum, 49, 155; J. Edenbrow, 9, 252; Mr and Mrs G. Ellison, 50, 53, 54, 56, 76, 77, 101, 115, 121, 132, 167, 171, 176, 205, 221, 225; Mr J. K. Elwood, 91, 199; Ermysted's Grammar School, 80; Dr G. C. Farnell, 11, 130, 157, 212, 218, 233, 250; Mrs M. Farnell, 26; Dr J. A. Farrer, 52, 117, 235; Giggleswick School, 78; Mrs L. Gill, 166; Mr Barry Greenwood/Times Newspapers, 175; Mr Barry Greenwood, 234; Mr J. Haines, 158, 159, 217; Mrs M. Haygarth, 168; Miss J. Hopper, 63; Mr C. Hollett, 164; Miss B. Horn, 113; Dr M. E. Howarth, 246; Mr M. Kirby, 144, 145; Mrs D. Lee, 75, 180, 214, 253; Leeds Reference Library, 139, 147; Mrs P. McEvoy, 204, 255; Mr J. Nelson, 114; Mrs P. Peacock, 223; Mrs M. Pullan, 116; Mr J. A. Rawcliffe, 183; Richmondshire Museum, 201, 239; Mrs C. J. Ritchie, 51; Mr T. Roberts, 100; Mr J. Robinson, 96, 213; Mrs E. M. Rowntree, 191; P. Sharp/Carr Family, 65; Mr W. Shields, 196; Mr A. Stockdale, 232; Mrs A. Sunter, 83, 220; Mr D. Swires, 200; Mrs G. Thompson/Ackrill Press, 254; Mrs J. Thompson, 85, 247; Miss M. Tunstall, 165; Mr E. Williamson, 59; Mr F. J. Willis, 47, 58, 99; Mrs J. Wiseman, 88, 238; Mr N. Whittall, 240; Mr D. Wood, 86, 181, 222; Mr E. I. Wright, 172; Yorkshire Archaeological Society, 236; Yorkshire Post 219; 126 photographs are by Marie Hartley and the rest from the Hartley/Ingilby archives. The title-page drawing of a Celtic brooch from Attermire Cave near Settle is reproduced by permission of the owner, Mr T. C. Lord. The photograph of the authors on the back jacket flap was taken by P. Tate.

I

· *Early man to the Middle Ages* ·

It is a sobering thought that the ancestors of modern man arrived in the Yorkshire Dales about 12,000 years ago, and that as we approach the second millennium AD, historic times only occupy some 2000 years. Early peoples used flint and stone for their weapons and tools, whereas we have invented nuclear fission.

The prolonged colonization of the dales follows a similar pattern to elsewhere, and evidence of early man was first found here when the Victoria Cave near Settle was excavated in the 1870s (plate 1). The finds included three bone implements now known to be of a type made by Upper Palaeolithic man dating from 10,000 BC.

Following these people came Mesolithic men, distinguished by their tiny flints called microliths found all over the dales. These folk were seasonal hunters and fishermen leading a precarious existence. Following them, Neolithic people arriving about 3500 BC lived a more settled life, keeping stock and clearing forests, but they left little except flints,

especially leaf-shaped arrow heads. Then came the Bronze Age people who buried their dead in stone circles as seen on Bordley Moor (949653) (plate 3), and near Yockenthwaite in Langstrothdale. Then again about 500 BC came the Iron Age people, the Celts, who when eventually threatened by the Romans formed the amalgamation of tribes known as the Brigantes. An aggressive people, they built fortifications, perhaps to defend tribal territories. The hill fort with nineteen huts surrounded by a massive wall on the summit of Ingleborough, Ta Dyke above Kettlewell on the way to Coverdale and other earthworks impress by their scale. Their villages and farms with hut circles and small square fields are innumerable on the hills, especially in Craven and on Greenber Edge, Addleborough, and Burton Moor, Penhill, in Wensleydale.

Significant place-names cluster round the last site: Penhill (British), Walden (Old English referring to Britons), and Thupton (Old Norse meaning 'giant'). Customs and legends have survived –

versions of real events distorted and romanticised over the centuries. The Burning of Bartle at West Witton feast is linked with the legend of a giant living on Penhill, and the well-known legend of Semerwater is a story found elsewhere in the folklore of Europe.

When the Romans advanced into Brigantian territory in AD 71, they met fierce resistance in the dales. But in time the Brigantes, led by Venutius who was the rejected husband of Cartimandua, their quisling queen, suffered defeat at their stronghold at Stanwick, north of Richmond. Venutius fled and his ultimate fate is unknown. Might he have taken refuge in Cotterdale, where in this hidden valley a sword and a finely wrought bronze scabbard of Celtic design were found in the last century? The conflict is a drama worthy of Naomi Mitchison who wrote *The Conquered* about Gaul.

In course of time Roman rule saw the native peoples become the Romano-British. The Romans opened up the dales. They built roads, a fort at Bainbridge, marching camps on Mastiles Lane, at Wensley and on Stainmore en route to Hadrian's wall. They introduced Christianity and brought stability for over three hundred years.

Whilst archaeologists using aerial photographs and trained observation have put much of these periods on record, excavation has been minimal in the dales where sites are not threatened by new buildings. Dr A. Raistrick pioneered prehistory in Craven; the Roman fort at Bainbridge has been explored by Leeds University, and recently sites near Reeth found by Sheffield University are beginning to reveal the extent of early occupation. A full sequence of pre-historic artifacts, from Neolithic to Iron Age, collected on the shores of Semerwater by Mr David Hall in the 1960s may be seen at the Dales Countryside Museum at Hawes.

In the next era – the Dark Ages or the Early Middle Ages, 500–1000 AD – invasions of Angles, Danes and Norsemen brought further change. The Angles, the English, introduced the open field system of agriculture and cultivations in strips, which on our steep hillsides were built up in terraces or lynchets suitable for ploughing by oxen, and which are now an outstanding feature of the landscape of the dales. These terraces may be seen to advantage near Conistone and Linton in Wharfedale, and between Carperby and Bolton Castle in Wensleydale (plate 18). The Danes reached the lower dales, and their settlements may be distinguished by the elements 'by' and 'thorpe'. It is the Norsemen coming from the west who left most impression. In the tenth century they colonised the upper dales and occupied high ground such as Dentdale, Grisedale and Malham Moor (see plate 8). The foundations of their long houses have been found in Kingsdale, at Ribblehead, Gunnerside and in Cragdale near Semerwater. In Kingsdale is Yordas cave, supposedly the haunt of a giant, another legend this time from the Vikings. It is they who named many of our villages and features of the landscape, such as Keld, gill and beck, and even left a legacy of characteristics and occasional facial resemblance of dalesfolk to some present-day Norwegians. These later groups brought their own traditions, languages and institutions, in particular Christianity and the establishment of the Celtic Church.

Finally we have the Norman Conquest in 1066 leading to the Middle Ages, 'a decisive turning-point in national development'. William of Normandy, bent on subduing it, devastated the north of England, took away their lands from the English and granted huge estates to his nobles, often his kinsmen. He introduced feudal tenure, consolidated the manorial system, and compiled Domesday Book for taxation purposes.

To this period we owe our castles and abbeys. The Norman lords began to build castles at once – Earl Alan at Richmond, his brother Ribald at Middleham and Robert de Romille at Skipton. Earl Alan built in stone and his great nephew erected the magnificent keep about 1170, whereas at Middleham the first building was a motte and bailey castle probably in wood. Middleham's importance rests on the fame of its later owners – the Nevilles and from 1471 to 1485 Richard Duke of Gloucester, who became Richard III. The Honour of Richmond and the Honour of Middleham were great feudal baronies administered by a multitude of officials. The lords hunted in the forests then covering much of the dales, but they also engaged in bloody wars. Richard Neville, Warwick the Kingmaker, was killed at Barnet in 1471 and Richard III at Bosworth in 1485 in the Wars of the Roses.

Skipton Castle has a different story;

for although it was started in Norman times, it was later rebuilt by the Cliffords, who were granted estates in Wharfedale and Westmorland, and in the seventeenth century it was restored by the famous Lady Anne Clifford. Bolton Castle is of later date. It stands up proudly on the north side of Wensleydale, begun by the Scropes in 1378, but its role was rather that of a fortified manor house than a castle. The imprisonment of Mary Queen of Scots for six months in 1568/9 lent it glamour. Although much smaller, Nappa Hall in Wensleydale and Walburn Hall near Downholme, Swaledale, are fortified manor houses of considerable interest. Nappa, starting as a pele tower, was built in 1459 by James Metcalfe, whose direct descendants lived there until 1756. The site of Walburn for human occupation is of great age and part of the house dates from the sixteenth century.

The link with France and the piety of the Normans and their followers introduced a new stage of manasticism, and the building of abbeys – Fountains, Jervaulx, Easby, Bolton and Coverham. The Cistercian order (Fountains and Jervaulx) was a splinter group of the Benedictines founded at Citeaux in Burgundy, whilst the Premonstratensian canons of Easby and Coverham took their name from Prémontré at Laon, France, and the canons at Bolton from St Augustine. Round Richmond especially, the patronage of Earl Alan and his knights, founded several small religious houses, including Marrick priory.

11

It was not a sacrifice for the great lords to give vast tracts of waste land in the dales to groups of monks in return for the salvation of their souls. Fountains was founded in 1132, by a rebel group from St Mary's Abbey, York; Jervaulx by the Normans from Richmond; Easby about 1155 by Roald, Constable of Richmond Castle, and Bolton Priory in 1151 by Alice de Romilly.

In the course of time, the magnificent abbey buildings rose up for the purpose of the worship of God, but also exhibited the splendour of Gothic architecture. The abbeys too were centres of commerce based on a system of granges scattered over their properties throughout the dales, where sheep and cattle were kept and reared, and whence issued dairy produce for home consumption and wool whose sale brought wealth.

The Pilgrimage of Grace and the Rising of the North are the culmination of this era. A little earlier in 1513 the Scots had invaded England. Dalesmen, whose horses were requisitioned, fought under the leadership of Cliffords and Scropes at Flodden Field, near Branxton in Northumberland, where in one day 10,000 Scots and 5000 English were slain. The horror of it still haunts the Field of Branxton.

By the sixteenth century, castles and abbeys began to undergo the disintegration of buildings outliving their purpose. Even by the time of the Wars of the Roses the days of the castle had passed and at the end of the Civil War castles were abandoned. As for the abbeys, monastic life became lax and in 1537/8 Henry VIII ordered the Dissolution of the Monasteries. What we see now are ruins robbed of their stones over the centuries, but none the less powerful images of a period of our history – the Middle Ages.

Prehistoric Sites

1 Victoria Cave (SD838650) at 1400 feet above sea level in Langcliffe Scar near Settle is the most important of the several bone caves found in Craven. It was discovered in 1838 (coronation year, hence its name), but was not scientifically excavated until the 1870s. The finds revealed the early arrival of modern man about 10,000 BC, and bones of animals pointed to different climates from cold to tropical over thousands of years (1958).

2 Semerwater off Wensleydale. The two so-called
Mermaid Stones from the bottom of the lake were
stranded here in the last Ice Age. Sheets of water were
sacred to prehistoric folk, and Semerwater was known
to people from the Neolithic Age onwards. In the last
century it was visited by rare birds, and it is now a
popular resort on a summer's day.

3 Bronze Age burial circle at Bordley out on the hills between Threshfield in Wharfedale and Malhamdale.

5 Maiden Castle on Harkerside, Swaledale, with a ditched enclosure of less than an acre and a passage shown here leading into it. The date of this important monument awaits excavation (1933).

4 Iron Age pit dwelling in Deepdale, Langstrothdale (1937).

Roman Road

6 Roman road up Buckden Raikes, Wharfedale, on the route from the Roman fort at Ilkley (Olicana) to the fort at Bainbridge. It took a different course here from that of the modern road, part of which was realigned in 1788. The old name, Kidstones Causey, implies that the road or parts of it were paved. At the summit of the pass the Roman road continued over the Stake Pass and past Semerwater to Bainbridge (1937).

Early Man and Dark Ages

7 Rey Cross or Rerecross on the summit of the Stainmore Pass, the A66. It was erected in the ninth century by King Edmund of Northumbria to mark the boundary between England and Strathclyde (part of the Lowlands and Cumbria). Stainmore is a historic route for Romans, Norsemen, drovers and now present-day traffic.

8 Viking Country. Capon Hall on Malham Moor, with Malham Tarn in the distance. It is one of the isolated farms which were originally Norse settlements.

9 Fountains Abbey, a base for granges in many parts of the dales.

10 Medieval stone causeway leading from Marrick Priory to Marrick village.

Castles

11 Richmond Castle was begun in 1071 by Earl Alan, and the magnificent keep, facing the great court, was erected about 1170.

12 Bolton Castle, Wensleydale, with in the foreground a June meadow (1950s).

13 Middleham Castle, Wensleydale, begun by Robert FitzRanulph, is historically the most important castle in the dales. In the fourteenth and fifteenth centuries it was held by the Nevilles, of whom Richard Earl of Warwick is called the 'King Maker', and then by Richard Duke of Gloucester, afterwards Richard III. The entrance approached over a moat and formerly a drawbridge is on the right, and the central keep looms. up on the left close to the curtain wall.

14 Skipton Castle, started by Robert de Romille in Norman times, was built in the early fourteenth and the seventeenth centuries by the famous Clifford family, who owned vast estates in the dales. It is closely associated with Lady Anne Clifford, who restored it after the Civil War. Above the doorway reached by steps seen on the left is a tablet recording the restoration made by her in 1659.

Manor Houses

15 Walburn Hall, near Downholme between Swaledale and Wensleydale, surrounded by medieval cultivation terraces. In the fourteenth century Walburn was a village with sixteen owners of tofts and bovates, and Beatrice Bellerby lived in what was then the hall. It is now early sixteenth century with an Elizabethan wing, and is protected by an embattled wall with a walkway. A huge chimney marks the site of the bakehouse (1930s).

16 The Old Hall at Grassington, Wharfedale, is reputedly the oldest inhabited house in Yorkshire. It was begun in the twelfth century by Nigel de Plumpton, on the site of an earlier house, and was added to in the next century. Over the years it has been greatly altered. Pevsner describes it as 'a remarkable survival'.

17 Nappa Hall, Wensleydale, built as a fortified manor house with pele tower, great hall, and a smaller tower, by James Metcalfe about 1459. It was the home of the famous family of Metcalfes until 1756. (Date unknown.)

18 Well-defined medieval lynchets in Malhamdale seen from a point a little beyond Gordale House, and on the right of the lynchets the remains of a small Iron Age farmstead, often seen above the strips of medieval ploughing. The hill beyond is Pikedaw.

19 Part of the fourteenth-century gatehouse, at
Kilnsey, Wharfedale, all that remains of the many
monastic buildings there when it was a grange of
Fountains Abbey. Kilnsey Old Hall behind now a barn,
was built by Christopher Wade in 1648.

II

· *The Living Past* ·

By the end of the Middle Ages, here taken to be the late sixteenth century, the pattern of settlement had been established. The towns of Richmond, Middleham, Skipton and Settle were all granted early charters for markets and fairs. Such is continuity that some market days fixed in the thirteenth century are still held on the same day of the week. But not all kept their status. Middleham was supplanted by Leyburn, Askrigg with a charter of 1587 by Hawes in 1700, and Reeth's market (1695) faded away as the lead-mines failed. Richmond at the foot of Swaledale circling a huge cobbled market-place is outstanding amongst English country towns.

Most villages are recorded in Domesday Book except at the heads of the dales, where permanent settlement in nucleated villages ceased at Reeth in Swaledale, Askrigg in Wensleydale and Kettlewell in Wharfedale. Above lay forest land difficult of access. The forest horn, still blown at night at Bainbridge in Wensleydale to guide travellers, is a relic of those days.

In the early Middle Ages it was a case of 'the rich man in his castle, the poor man at his gate', except for the lords of the manors or officials who built comparatively large houses (plate 17). One-roomed hovels for peasants were of timber, while modest single-storied houses for tenants and small farmers were often cruck-built and ling- or rush-thatched with central hearths and holes in the roof for smoke. Chimneys and smoke hoods came later. Few buildings constructed with the pairs of curved upright timbers called crucks survive in the dales, except for a few barns near Bolton Abbey in Wharfedale. Early farmhouses were often longhouses, that is buildings occupied by the farmer's family at one end and by his cows at the other under one roof. Again no complete example of this ancient tradition is to be seen in the dales. Agill, above the Valley of Desolation at Bolton Abbey, single-storied and formerly ling-thatched, is the nearest.

One period above all – the seventeenth century – marked important change with lasting effect. Following the Dissolution of the Monasteries the vast monastic properties, granted away or sold and attracting speculators, resulted in fragmentation and individual ownership of separate farms. Similarly the Lordship of Middleham, crown property, led to the same process because of Charles I's debts, and other comparable events elsewhere spread ownership.

So we have the boom in building in stone beginning in the late sixteenth century and lasting throughout the seventeenth. These yeomen's houses with mullion windows, dated doorheads, stone arched fireplaces, sometimes panelling and plasterwork, adorn the dales scene. The yeomen filled their houses with oak furniture (plates 41–2) and shortly with grandfather clocks made in the dales. But two centuries later fashion dictated lighter appointments and oak furniture was sold to antique dealers. Today it is rare indeed to find the full complement of the yeoman's or the statesman's furniture, some of it as described by Adam Sedgwick. Other equipment included a cheese press, a beef loft for drying pickled beef, a bakestone for baking oatcake, and bee boles for beehives for honey for sweetening.

Over the next centuries houses large and small continued to be built and rebuilt, often on the same sites. Sometimes Georgian fronts were superimposed on seventeenth-century houses. Georgian houses with small-paned sash windows were followed by plainer Victorian houses, all of which blend harmoniously in the village street. Seen in every dale, isolated farmhouses, often built in the late eighteenth or early nineteenth century, have an adjoining barn or barns alongside, but not with the cow byre next to the house. We call them laithe-houses from the Old Norse *hlaða*, a laithe or barn. Students of vernacular architecture have classified types of houses in groups using technical terms.

It is well known that the names of people were derived from their occupations or the places where they were born. Their names appear in tax returns, musters, rentals and rate books. In early days they moved about more than we might expect, and even now it is usually regarded as more advantageous to move southwards. There is seldom long continuity on a farm. Certain names of old families belonged, and often still do, to specific places or dales. Mention the name Hird, and we should expect them to live in or have come from Arkengarthdale. We remember in the 1930s the Knowles of Halton Gill, whose forelders were tenants of Fountains Abbey. So numerous are the Metcalfes of Wensleydale and the Aldersons of Swaledale, now spread all over the world, that they have formed societies of their own.

Everyone spoke dialect, so little heard now. Characters who behaved regardless of other people's opinions have gone, and 'Old Standards' – the elders of a village looked up to for advice – no longer exist. The influx of newcomers, the influence of better education and all-pervading television have had their effect. The photographs in this book bring back some of these staunchly independent people of former generations.

Places

20 Richmond from the top of the castle keep looking down into the cobbled market-place with the market cross (obelisk), Holy Trinity church and behind it the tower of Greyfriars. Richmond is a medieval town with a veneer of Georgian and Victorian building superimposed on it. Since this photograph was taken in the 1950s the hillsides behind have been covered with houses and the market-place itself packed with motor cars and buses. Nevertheless, Richmond is the finest small town in the north of England.

21 Reeth, Swaledale, formerly a market town with four fairs and a market on Fridays, was a centre for the dale in the lead-mining days. Crowded with visitors in the summer, it has a large agricultural show and many local activities (1981).

22 Yockenthwaite, one of the hamlets in Langstrothdale, whose peculiar name is derived from an Old Irish personal name Eogan. In medieval days it was a lodge in the forest, and when this photograph was taken in 1937, it was the home of the Hirds and the Beresfords.

23 Gunnerside, Swaledale, in winter, a
Norse settlement and later a centre for lead-
miners (1950s).

24 Halton Gill at the head of Littondale, at
the foot of the Horsehead Pass from
Langstrothdale (1986).

Houses

25 Worton Hall, Wensleydale, built by Anthony Besson in 1600. He with other leading men was the founder of Yorebridge Grammar School between Askrigg and Bainbridge.

26 Hill Top, Malham, dated 1617, built by William Preston, a typical seventeenth-century yeoman's house.

27 Blackburn Hall near the church at Grinton, Swaledale, an old house altered in 1635. It possibly stands on the site of the chief house of Bridlington Priory, which was granted the manor of Grinton by Walter de Gant, and it is named after the Blackburn family of Richmond, who owned it in the eighteenth century.

28 Stainforth Hall at Knight or Little Stainforth, Ribblesdale. One of the larger yeomen's houses in the dales, it was built by Samuel Watson, a Quaker, in 1672. In 1774 it was owned by Christopher Weatherhead, merchant of Liverpool, who had plantations in the West Indies (1950s).

29 Woodhouse Manor between Burnsall and Appletreewick, Wharfedale, now an isolated farm and barns, but formerly a village and manor belonging to the Priory of Marton-in-Cleveland. This charming seventeenth-century house was for generations the home of the Blands (1960s).

30 Dougill Hall, near Summerbridge, Nidderdale, dated IDE 1722. It takes its name from a local family who were tenants of Fountains Abbey. It has a stone arched fireplace composed of three stones, a keystone and two long stones incised to simulate small ones.

31 Coleby Hall on Abbotside, Wensleydale, built by John Coleby in 1655. As one of the later speculators in monastic property, John Coleby's father acquired a third of the Manor of Wensleydale (Abbotside). The hall has three fine arched fireplaces. It has been divided into two, and is now the home of the family of a twentieth-century yeoman.

32 Owlcotes or Oldcotes, Littondale, a yeoman's house w the initials and date ISMS 1650 over the door.

33 Kisdon farm (east) above Muker, Swaledale, formerly a typical small dales farm. Early in the nineteenth century it was the home of a branch of the Fawcett family, one of whom Ralph (b. 1787) married twice and had twelve children. Some of these emigrated to America and settled at Dubuque, Iowa. The house is now a country cottage (1985).

34 Levy Pool, a ling-thatched house and barns near Bowes on the Pennine Way, dated 1736. It was last occupied by Mr and Mrs J. Addison in 1925. It is still there in a ruinous state, and is the best surviving example of ling thatching in the dales (c. 1965).

Features of Houses

35 Fireplace at the Old Hall, Thoralby, Bishopdale, built in 1641. The hall has two arched fireplaces recently uncovered. This one is particularly refined workmanship.

36 Beautifully arched bee boles at Spen House, Abbotside, Wensleydale. Bee boles for beehives for a supply of honey for sweetening may be found here and there near farmhouses. Usually they are square or upright alcoves in walls.

37 Bakestone alongside the fireplace and thus sharing the flue at Padside Hall, Nidderdale. Very many farmhouses in the old West Riding dales had built-in bakestones for baking thin oatcake (1966).

38 Round stone cheese press at Brimham Lodge, Nidderdale, probably seventeenth century.

39 The doorway of Ellerbeck, Bowland, with the initials and date WIS IS 1694. The design resembles that of one of the doorways of Askrigg Old Hall, destroyed by fire in 1935.

40 A disused two-seater privy at Park House, Bordley, in a small eighteenth-century building attached to the back of the house. We have been told of a four-seater privy now gone in Wensleydale (1989).

Furnishings

41 Oak court cupboard typical of the furniture in the yeomen's houses in the dales in the seventeenth century. This one has the initials and date carved on it ADA 1684. We once saw three court cupboards, two of which had the same initials as the then owners, in a farmhouse in Dentdale.

42 Seventeenth-century oak dresser with rack from Wharfedale (1966).

43 Oak spoon rack and Bible box from Nidderdale.

44 A Nidderdale grandfather clock with a silver and brass dial made by Will Snow of Padside about 1763. There were several members of the Snow family of clockmakers, many at Otley, beginning in 1664.

45 A Nidderdale sampler worked by Judith Raynor aged nine, dated May 14th 1837, and with the words at the bottom, 'By this you see how kind my parents is to me'.

46 Wash-handstand complete with toilet accessories: ewer and handbasin, soap dish, sponge holder, tooth brush holder, chamber pot and slop pail (1989).

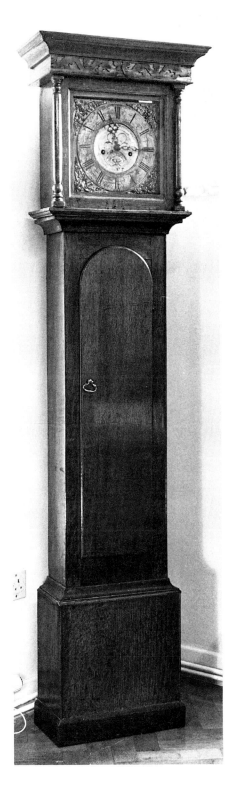

Wedding Groups

47 A group at the Quaker wedding of Matthew Willis of Carperby and Jane Heather Jacob from Ireland at Cartmel meeting house on 12 August 1909. The venue for the wedding was chosen as central for the families. Standing on the left are Matthew and Jane with other members of the Willis and Jacob families.

48 Group outside the farmhouse, Rycroft, on the main Clapham to Ingleton road, at the wedding of Grace Wilshaw and Charlie Capstick, a farmer. His father, Willie Capstick (first on the right in a top hat), was the blacksmith at Clapham (c. 1907).

49 Group at the wedding of John Cherry of Reeth, Swaledale, and Margaret Banks of Askrigg, Wensleydale, at Askrigg about 1890. On the right of the bride are Nelly Hunter (Storey) and Hannah Banks. Behind the bridegroom are Canon C. Whaley, vicar of Askrigg, and Sarah Banks (mother) in white cap.

50 The wedding group of Maribell Allen and Jack Harris, headmaster of Cowgill School, at Lamb Parrock, Dentdale, in the late 1880s. On the left is the Rev. Robert Pickering, vicar of Cowgill.

Families

53 Jim and Jane Ellison in the doorway of Greenwell, Dent. When they married, they went to Liverpool as cowkeepers, but the climate did not suit Jim so they returned. Jane's father retired, and they took over his farm, Greenwell, on the south side of Dentdale (1908).

54 John and Mary Middleton, who lived at Laning, Dent Town. John was a joiner (1912).

51 The King family and staff at the Mount, West Burton, Wensleydale, about 1910. Back row from left to right: Jack Sayer, Ethel Pearson, Nellie Heseltine? (cook), Alice Pearson, 'Shady' Pearson. Seated: Walter Henry King, Florence Muriel King, William Robinson King, and William Bernard Robinson King (Woodwardian Professor of Geology at Cambridge 1843–1955 FRS).

52 The Farrers, lawyers and bankers, settled in Clapham in the seventeenth century, and in 1841 built Ingleborough Hall. Although not in the direct line, Dr J. A. Farrer now owns the manor and lives in the village. The hall, sold in 1952, is an outdoor centre for school children. The group includes James Anson Farrer (*standing*) and his wife of Ingleborough Hall (early 1890s).

55 The family of William (1807–69) and Mary Mawer (1809–97), all born at Braidley, Coverdale. William came from Heathen Carr near Lodge, Nidderdale, and Mary from Swineside, Gammersgill, Coverdale. They had ten children, two of whom died young, and a daughter Mary, not in the photograph. This was taken at Riverside, Gammersgill, where Joseph (1852–1924, *centre back*) farmed (c. 1910).

56 Alice Allen, née Bayne, of Cowgill, married George Allen
and went to live at Ewegales farm, Dentdale, where they
had six children. George died young. When the boys
were old enough, they moved to a larger sheep farm,
Whiteindales, near Clitheroe in Bowland, and later went to
Broughton Fields near Skipton. Alice lived to be over ninety.

57 (*Right*) William Wallbank, born in 1904 at Keasden Head near Clapham, a large sheep farm. As a young man William farmed Rantree where he still lives. He married and has six children, and is now retired. He has a fund of tales of old times, and told us that at Keasden Head they could sit seventy down to dinner (1989).

58 (*Above*) Maria Willis (1840–1925) was a Barker from Crosby Garrett, Cumbria. She married Thomas Willis, junior, of Manor House, Carperby, son of the famous Shorthorn breeder. He died in 1892. Her eldest son died of tuberculosis in 1893 when her second son was only ten. She farmed on her own for fifteen years, and a great cheesemaker, she expanded the cheese-making into a considerable business (1893/4).

59 Young Bill, Bill Ingleby (1898–1969), at Nether Hesleden, Littondale. He was head shepherd at Cover Head for twenty years then shepherd at Penyghent farm, and for twenty years lived at Nether Hesleden looking after the sheep there until he was seventy, when he became odd job man. He was a fount of local country lore (1968).

Farming Families

60 Stephen and Eliza Carr (née Horner) at Park House, Bordley, near Malhamdale. They were married in September 1873, and had eleven children, five boys and six girls. Eliza holds the baby Elizabeth known as Daisy, and Nanny, the eldest girl, is on the horse (1890s).

61 The family of Anthony and Annas Scott at High Frith above West Stonesdale, upper Swaledale. *From left to right:* Maggie holding Dick's hand, Jinnie, John, Annas, young Anthony and Anthony on Daisy. In 1864 Annas, then Annas Hunter, worked a fine sampler and she is remembered as keeping 100 geese. John and Anthony became policemen in Burnley. The house, built in 1876 by Anthony Scott has been derelict for many years (1890s).

62 A party of Hawes ladies, probably members of a Church of England group: *Back row from left to right*: Mrs Anderton (wife of the doctor), Mrs J. Heseltine, Mrs R. Iveson, Mrs 'Bobby' Knowles, Mrs Ann Dinsdale (Gayle), Mrs J. Iveson, Mrs Herrington, Mrs D. D. Atkinson, Mrs K. Moore. *Middle row*: Mrs Bates (School House), Mrs Bob Spencer, ?, ?, Mrs T. Hiscock, Mrs Broderick, Mrs Bell, Mrs J. Wilson, Mrs F. Martland, Mrs J. Mason. *Front row*: Mrs J. Moore (coal merchant), Miss Clarkson (Board Hotel), Mrs (Doctor) Richardson,

Mrs Ellwood (vicar's wife), Mrs E. Broughton (Lord Wharncliffe's agent, Burn House) Mrs C. Iveson, Mrs Metcalfe, Mrs P. Webster. (Early twentieth century).

63 A group at Askrigg of whom a few are known – Aaron Knaggs *on the left*, Tom Lodge with pipe, W. Metcalfe *far right and behind him* J. Horner.

Present-day Dales Families

64 A dales family: Allen and Jennifer Kirkbride with Maria, Ian and Rachael and Tilly the cat at Town Head farm, Askrigg.

65 The Carr family at Lee Gate, Malham. *From left to right*: Norman, Florence, Frank (senior), Frank (junior). *Seated*: Christine with Robert and Jane with Harriet.

III

· *Religion · Education ·*

It goes without saying that the oldest buildings in the villages and towns of the dales are usually the churches. Very many have a twelfth-century core and sometimes a Norman font. Later generations of men rebuilt them or added a tower or aisles, often in the Perpendicular period. Some were heavily restored or rebuilt in the last century. They are the focal point of a village round which it originally grew and are to be cherished.

It has to be admitted that the churches of the dales when compared with others elsewhere in Yorkshire are not outstanding. In the Middle Ages wealth was drawn out of the area to build the abbeys. But they have many points of interest. Aysgarth, West Witton, Coverham and Middleham have fragments of Anglian crosses, and Burnsall has Anglo-Danish hogbacks pointing to a pre-Conquest foundation. Easby, pre-dating Easby Abbey alongside it, has thirteenth-century frescoes and a replica of the Easby Cross (the original is in the Victoria and Albert Museum). There is

remarkable woodwork: the rood-loft at Hubberholme which because of its remote position survived the edict for their destruction at the Reformation; the magnificent rood screens at Wensley and Aysgarth, the one from Easby Abbey and the other probably from Jervaulx; poppyheads, the work of the Ripon carvers dating from about 1510 in the same churches; and stalls at St Mary's, Richmond; a rood screen at Holy Trinity, Skipton.

After the Reformation, as is well known, harsh regulations suppressed Catholicism. The saying of Mass was prohibited, as the priest's hiding holes at Ripley Castle and Lawkland Hall testify. The numbers of Recusants, that is people usually Catholics not attending the established church, were reported in Archdeacons' Visitations. None the less, restrictions were eventually lifted, and there are a number of Roman Catholic churches and schools in the dales.

To turn to Nonconformity, the general movement of Dissent starting in Elizabethan times developed in the north into groups of Independents and Seekers who were dissatisfied with the church and sought new forms of worship. Starting humbly by meeting in cottages, Nonconformist sects progressed so that chapels and meeting houses were built to become part of the fabric of villages and towns. The Independents, who turned into the Congregationalists, were oppressed by a series of acts passed in the 1660s, hence the tradition in Swaledale of a secret meeting place at Swinnergill Kirk (plate 70). Encouraged by Lord Wharton, they built their first chapel at Low Row in 1691.

Covering a similar period, the Seekers led to the formation of the Quakers. George Fox, the founder, visited Wensleydale, Wharfedale, Garsdale and Dent in 1652. Quakers too, who were regarded as political offenders, suffered for their faith, and for non-payment of tithes some were imprisoned. The earliest meeting house, Brigflatts near Sedbergh, built in 1674, is a place of pilgrimage.

The third strand of dissent, Wesleyan Methodism, began in the eighteenth century when John Wesley journeyed into Swaledale in 1761 and found a society already established there. As congregations increased, small chapels gave way to larger as at Airton in Airedale, where a chapel built in 1833 was followed by a larger one in 1896. Turned into houses or barns, these early chapels are mute reminders of dedicated effort.

Other breakaway groups became established for a time. The Barkerites built a chapel, now a house, at Eskeleth in Arkengarthdale. There was a Sandemanian chapel at Gayle near Hawes,

and at Thornton Rust in Wensleydale were a Calvinist chapel and a Particular Baptist, all of which have gone.

The role of schools has much in common with that of churches. They were founded with endowments by men, often clerics, who saw a need for education in their native places. There were chantry schools in the fifteenth century at Sedbergh, Giggleswick, Richmond and Skipton, all of which were re-founded as free grammar schools in the mid 1550s. Ermysted's at Skipton adopted the name of the founder. The seventeenth century saw other endowed grammar schools started at Askrigg in 1601, Dent in 1604, Burnsall in 1605 (plate 81), Kirkby Malham in 1606, Halton Gill in 1630, Arkengarthdale in 1659, and many more.

These schools passed through phases usually dependent on the quality of the masters, and they have developed differently. Sedbergh and Giggleswick are now the great public boarding schools of the dales, the one a boys' school and the other admitting girls of all ages in 1983. Richmond Grammar School joined up with the Girls High School and the County Modern to become Richmond School in 1971, whilst Ermysted's for boys is now a Voluntary Aided School. These all have close links with Oxford and Cambridge colleges.

It is noticeable that none of these schools originally provided for girls, who remained illiterate longer than boys. There were dame schools in most villages, where besides simple lessons boys and girls were taught to knit. Other day and boarding schools were started up for girls. In the 1850s for example were the Misses Gibbin's and Wilson's establishment at Settle, and the Richmond Institution for 'Young Ladies' at Richmond. There were also schools like Dotheby's Hall for boys which were exposed by Dickens clustered in the Bowes–Teesdale region;

In 1811, following the foundation of a society promoting education in the Church of England, National Schools were built, two being at Hawes and Grassington. These as well as Sunday Schools spelled the beginning of the end of illiteracy for the poor which lingered on with the elderly up to 100 years ago. Then came the great Elementary Education Act of 1870 by which school boards were formed and the Victorian school buildings familiar to us rose up, and later Acts altered the course of education. Alas, depopulation has meant the closing of many small schools. Lunds at the head of Wensleydale, which closed in 1945, once had fifty-six pupils. Similarly for the same reason and the falling off in church attendance, parishes have been joined and vicars serve several churches. We have often noted that outstanding vicars, ministers and school teachers are remembered with gratitude and affection long after they have gone.

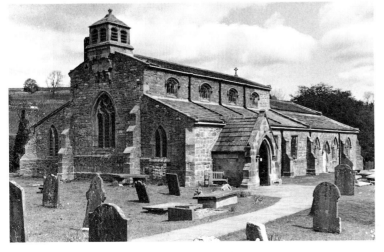

66 Hubberholme church in Langstrothdale dating from the twelfth century and famous for its rood loft. Across the bridge is the George Inn at the foot of Kirkgill.

67 Linton church between Linton and Grassington and close to the river Wharfe, interesting for its Norman work. 'A delightful little church' (Pevsner).

Church Interiors

68 The magnificent rood screen in Aysgarth church, Wensleydale, 35 feet long, gilded and painted in reds, greens and blues. It dates from about 1510 (1989).

69 Two of the eight poppy-heads in Wensley church attributed to the Ripon Carvers, early sixteenth century. Each has a different animal, and these depict one biting its tail, and one behind a hare with carved fur but missing an ear.

Nonconformity

70 Swinnergill Kirk, upper Swaledale, where a narrow cave extends under the waterfall. It is traditionally associated with Dissenters, who met here to worship in secret.

71 Countersett Quaker meeting house near Semerwater built by Michael Robinson about 1710. It was repaired and altered in 1778/9. It has been used by Primitive Methodists and the Methodists, whilst Friends moved to Bainbridge meeting house (D. S. Hall) (c. 1950).

72 Barkerite chapel at Eskeleth, Arkengarthdale, built in the 1840s, or 1850s. This was one of the sects breaking away from Methodism founded by Joseph Barker (1806–75) who visited the dales.

73 Gunnerside chapel, Swaledale, built in 1867. The photograph was taken on the first Sunday in July, the Midsummer Festival, when the chapel was once crowded to overflowing (1989).

74 Harvest Festival at Askrigg Moor Road Primitive Methodist chapel, built in 1869. The chapel closed in 1971 and is now two houses.

Festivities

75 Middlesmoor Sunday School outing to Woodale up the valley below Scar in upper Nidderdale. The vicar is the Rev. K. W. Summerfield (c. 1900).

76 The Dent Dale United Band of Hope Demonstration on 20 August 1907. They were in fancy dress to represent the evils of drink. The Band of Hope was started in 1847 by a group of young people pledged not to drink alcohol, and was usually associated with church or chapel.

77 Children playing a round game at a Sunday School party
held annually in the vicarage croft at Dent Town about 1900.

Schools

78 Gigglleswick School near Settle, originally founded in 1553 by a royal charter as a free grammar school, has developed over the centuries into a well-known public school. It has links with Christ's and St John's Colleges, Cambridge, and Queen's College, Oxford.

79 In 1971 Richmond School absorbed Richmond Grammar School, founded in 1567. The new school, seen in the photograph, was built in 1851, and is now where some 220 eleven-year olds, including some from Swaledale, spend their first year of secondary education (1989).

80 Ermysted's Grammar
School, Skipton, was re-founded
by William Ermysted in 1548.
New buildings were erected in
1876, and boys from the dales are
given priority for admittance.

81 Burnsall Grammar School
and school master's house was
built and endowed in 1605 by Sir
William Craven, alderman of
London. The upper storey,
divided into chambers, is the
original dormitory for boarders.
Girls were admitted about 1853.
It is now a primary school (1937).

Classrooms

82 A classroom at Richmond Girls High School in 1940. This was a teaching and seminar room used largely by the fifth and sixth formers. The school was newly-built to an advanced design by D. Clarke-Hall in 1938/9, and is now part of Richmond School (*see* Pevsner).

83 Selside School, Ribblesdale, in 1944. There were nine pupils who walked sometimes three miles to school. *Sitting on the front desk*: Margaret Wilcock, Arthur Wilcock and Bobby Shepherd. *Middle desk*: Norah Sunter, Eileen Sunter and Lena Newhouse. *Back desk*: Shirley Morphet, Betty Shepherd and Margaret Towler. The school closed in 1956.

School Transport

84 Frank Carr, whose home was and still is at Lee Gate, Malham Moor, went the three miles to Malham School on Neddy. His sister, Bessie, is holding the donkey, and his mother, Caroline Carr, and his sister, Doris, are in the doorway (1928).

85 Doris Carr (now Mrs J. Thompson) and the children of Malham Tarn School, where she taught from 1930 to 1942. Miss Carr at first stayed there during weekdays, then walked home each night to Lee Gate on Malham Moor until her father provided her with a pony. In 1930 there were ten children and in 1942 three, shortly after which the school closed.

86 School taxi owned by H. Wood and Sons of Bolton Abbey, taking Barden children home from school at Beamsley (c. 1937).

School Groups

87 Horsehouse School, Coverdale, in 1907. Miriam Moorhouse (seen at the back of the group) was head teacher from 1894 to 1910, helped by her elder sister. She had been trained at Whitelands College, London, taught everything, and was highly respected (c. 1907).

88 Kettlewell had an early school built by Solomon Swale, but in the mid-nineteenth century, owing to a dispute between church and chapel, a school board was formed and a new board school, the present one north of the village, was built and opened in 1885. William L. Carradice, seen in the doorway, was the first master (1898). (E. Raistrick.)

89 Arncliffe Church of England school, Littondale, built as a National School in 1848, and later rebuilt. Since the closure of Litton and Halton Gill schools all the children in Littondale under the age of eleven attend Arncliffe. There are now twenty-two pupils (1989).

IV

· The Farming Scene ·

The story of farming in the dales is a long one, and continuity is the theme: sheep shears are still of a similar pattern to those used in the Iron Age; the names of different parts of a barn – *boskins*, *skelbuse* – come from the Norsemen, and the traditional length of a barn stems from the 'bay', about sixteen feet, which accommodates four cows, the same number as a yoke of oxen which once pulled the plough (Addy).

Arable fields, as we have described in Chapter I, once surrounded the villages, except those at the heads of the dales. They were part of the manorial system with its boon works, officials and manor courts. Each man had strips in the fields and in proportion cattle gates (rights) in the cow pastures above the villages and stints for sheep on the moors. Alongside this, monastic farming on a grand scale tamed wild country. The monks had sheep houses and their cheese was made from ewes' milk, two practices only now being revived in the dales. They salved sheep with tar and butter, a method superseded by dipping in the last century, and they established a pattern of settlement in which their granges eventually became farms and hamlets which are still there.

About 1600, a date varying considerably in different places, a revolution occurred: strips in the arable fields were walled round in blocks to make closes, which can be seen today as irregular-shaped fields round villages. A wholly pastoral type of farming with mixed stock was established in the upper dales. There followed a century of progress. The gentry bred horses; the yeomen banded together to keep bulls 'of good breed' communally; as land was reclaimed small farmers increased in numbers; tradesmen, innkeepers, shopkeepers had little farms. Labourers were the largest group, and servants, both male and female, were hired by the year. Barns, matching the yeomen's houses in style, were built in Wharfedale, Littondale and Malhamdale. Forest land was disappearing and modern farming beginning.

In the eighteenth century turnpike

roads opened up the country and rec-lamation of moors continued. (One such area, Greenfield, above Beckermonds, mentioned by Arthur Young, is now afforested.) Then came the enclosures of the cow pastures created by agreement or by individual acts of parliament in this and the nineteenth century. In the dales, enclosure was beneficial in solving disputes over boundaries and allowing selective stock-breeding. A spate of building of barns followed. The tracks once made by the cows being driven down from the pastures can still be seen, and the new walls dividing up the allot-ments, planned on paper in straight lines, changed the face of the landscape. Some of these walls built up steep hill-sides are cause for marvel (plate 130).

The monks used to visit their granges on ambling mares, and later the indus-trial era created a huge demand for pack-horses – a type similar to the Fell pony of Cumbria and often indiscriminately called Galloways. In modern times Dales ponies are the local breed, slightly larger than the Fell. Depending on size, farms had from two to four horses. 'You had to have one for a backwatch', and farmers competed as to who had the best pony. Others enjoyed breaking in *stags* (young horses): 'I've known us break as many as four horses in one winter, work as well. But we didn't think about work i' them days.'

Cattle meanwhile were being im-proved by Robert Bakewell (1725–1795) of Longhorn fame, and his disciples, the Colling and Booth brothers, per-fected the Beef Shorthorn in competi-tion with Bates of Kirklevington.

The quality of their stock was displayed by such animals as the Craven and Aire-dale Heifers and the Durham Ox, which travelled round the country. Notable dales breeders of Shorthorns were the Willises of Carperby, the Carrs of Stackhouse near Settle, and the Garths of Swaledale. The Shorthorns reigned supreme at home and overseas.

By 1905, however, milk production was more favoured, and local breeders allied themselves with the Dairy Short-horn Association and in 1944 the North-ern Dairy Shorthorns. But by the mid 1950s these had been engulfed through-out the dales by the black-and-white Friesians which gave more milk. Nowa-days increasing numbers of imported cattle – Limousin and Charolais – are being kept.

In the sheep world we have both long-woolled and short-woolled sheep – the Teeswater and Wensleydale with their long lustrous wool kept on lower ground, and the Swaledale, Dalesbred and Rough Fell with coarse wool and horns *heughed* on the hills in their own areas. The Cistercians, incidentally, kept short-woolled sheep (Power). In 1756, accord-ing to tithe records, there were 2191 cows and 22,609 sheep in the original parish of Aysgarth, that is upper Wensleydale. Swaledales are now wide-spread and the tups command large prices. The Teeswaters and Wensleydales are used for crossing with the Swaledales, and these crosses are bought by lowland farmers; for the role of the dales has been and is a rearing ground for stock.

From about 1860 mowing machines pulled by horses replaced scythes for

cutting grass to make hay – a small revolution in itself. Auction marts did away
with fairs in market-places. Formerly,
horses in the northernmost dales were
often bought at Brough Hill Fair, which
was preceded by Hawes Fair and by
Cowper Day at Kirkby Stephen. (The
nuns of Marrick Priory sold cattle at
Brough in 1415.) Agricultural shows
were started, that at Hawes in 1843. The
railways arrived to carry goods and milk
swiftly, and dairies were opened for the
manufacture of cheese.

The last revolution since the Second
World War has been the introduction
of electricity, so that milking cows and
clipping sheep by hand has almost
ceased. More important was the change
from horses as motive power to tractors,
when the age-old wooden sledges,
sweeps, coups and carts were
abandoned. Tractors are labour-saving
and the workforce in consequence has
diminished. They pull the new disc
mowers, balers, acrobats for strewing
hay, muck spreaders and so on. As a
result at haytime the new machines
together with the widespread making of
silage have overcome dependence on the
weather. But they are expensive and
have altered the economics of dales
farms. Subsistence farming has gone.
Small farms with poor roads in remote
valleys are joined up with big farms, and
the houses occupied as holiday cottages,
with the result that there is little scope
for young men wishing to start farming.
Also slumps such as that of the 1930s
and bad winters have not helped. Not
only that but the field barns, such a
feature of the dales, have become redundant as large new buildings attracting
government grants replace them. Walls
too are in jeopardy because of the
smaller work force and rising costs, and
the over-fertilised meadows have lost
their variety of flowers. But Environ-
mentally Sensitive Areas are being promoted, so that some farmers, especially
in Swaledale, are adopting traditional
methods of farming and saving the
flowery meads.

Fairs

90 Askrigg Hill Fair, started about 1785 with a few lots of sheep, was first held at various locations. Early in the last century it was established on Fair Allotment above Askrigg, and became a well-known event, attracting stock, gipsies and crowds of people. The fair gradually diminished and ended in the 1930s (c. 1900).

91 The annual Skipton Horse Fair held in the High Street in August after haytime. Some of these horses were called July Razors. The fair finished soon after this photograph was taken in the early 1930s.

92 A string of horses wait patiently at Brough Hill Fair (1950s).

93 Gipsies from the Borders at Brough Hill Fair, near Warcop, Cumbria. The matriarch is surrounded by her family, whilst the men are elsewhere trading in horses. The fair dates back to 1331 and is described in 1829 as the largest in the North of England. Brough Hill was the celebrated fair to which farmers from the dales resorted to sell or buy horses.

94 Appleby Fair in Cumbria, held on Gallows Hill; a photograph taken about 1950 before the motorised trailers of the gipsies and potters began to overtake caravans in numbers. Appleby New Fair was instituted in 1750, and is held in early June.

95 Whip and harness seller at Appleby Fair (c. 1950).

Horses

96 Swaledale sheep being driven across the water splash on the Oxnop Pass, Swaledale. This is now bridged over (1920s).

97 Potters, camping here for a day or two on their way to Appleby Fair, water their horses at Arngill above Askrigg, Wensleydale. This water splash was covered over and the wooden bridge removed in the 1950s (1942).

98 Dewpond above Grassington, Wharfedale. There are many dewponds in the limestone country of the Yorkshire Dales; some are medieval and a few were made in the late nineteenth century. They were hollowed out, lined with a mixture containing clay and paved to prevent hooves sinking in (1937). (Raistrick.)

Shorthorns

99 The prize-winning bull, Vice Admiral, from the Shorthorn herd of Thomas Willis (1791–1887) of Carperby, Wensleydale. The oil painting was painted by A. M. Gauci, whose sisters filled in the background. From 1877 to 1881 Vice Admiral was exhibited at five successive royal shows all over the country, and won four first prizes and in 1881 the Shorthorn championship.

100 Some of the Tipperthwaite Northern Dairy Shorthorn herd at Close House farm, Giggleswick. The nucleus of the herd came from two female calves given as a wedding present to T. Dawson Bilsborough and his wife, Ella. They started farming in 1920 at Wham, then Tosside, and finally at Giggleswick. The herd was sold in 1958 (1956).

101 A herd of Dairy Shorthorn cows being driven to Hill Top farm, Deepdale, Dentdale, by the farm man, Jack Thompson. The farmer at Hill Top was W. Mason (late 1930s).

Milk

102 Milking on the pastures in Swaledale, perhaps at Muker. Up to the 1920s milking out of doors in summer was usual. Here the milk is being carried to the farmhouse in two backcans on a crate on a pony. A backcan held up to eight gallons.

103 Frank Thackray milking at Park House, Bordley.

104 Field Barns of Malham West on the lane to the former open fields. There are four barns here, one just glimpsed behind the middle one and a ruin on the right (1989).

105 A well-built cattle creep on Park House farm, Bordley. These structures allowed cattle to gain access from fields without water to fields which had it. This one crosses underneath a road. They are not unusual but are not common. Four, some dilapidated, cross the road from Skyrethorns near Threshfield towards Bordley.

106 A once familiar sight – a milk stand for milk cans collected when full and deposited when empty by lorries, here seen at Countersett, Wensleydale (1950s). Tankers collecting milk in bulk now visit each farm (*see* plate 229).

Sheep and Lambs

107 Dick Hodgson bringing Swaledale ewes and lambs back to the moor up the moor road, Askrigg, after lambing at Lowlands Farm, Askrigg (1950s).

108 Swaledale sheep waiting to be fed in March 1989 against a background of Ribblehead Viaduct and Whernside.

109 Mr A. Greenbank counting sheep as they come off Blea Moor (1967).

110 Frank Carr with Dalesbred ewes and lambs in front of a sheep house at Lee Gate, Malham Moor. This, built in 1984, was the first in that area. It holds 500 ewes in pens. The sheep spend one or two days in individual pens to lamb and are then let out a very few at a time (1989).

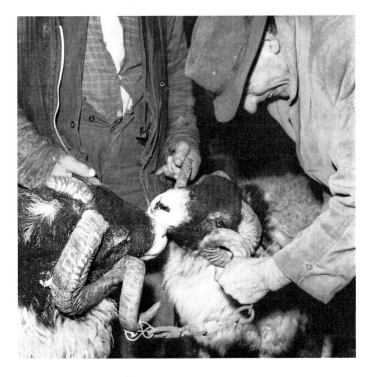

111 Cherry and George Kearton fastening a chain to the horns of two Swaledale tups at Thwaite, Swaledale. A hole is drilled through one of each tup's horns. Thus attached together they cannot stray or jump walls before tupping time in November. This practice is recorded in Dent in 1794 (1967).

Among the Sheep

112 Sheep salving at a farm in Wensleydale, whereabouts and date unknown. Salving was the age-old practice to prevent scab and other diseases before dipping was introduced. It faded out during the latter half of the last century.

113 Dipping sheep from Castle Bank farm in Apedale, off Wensleydale. The group of eight men includes Robert Horn on the left, Tom Metcalfe in the centre, Albert Spensley looking up on the right, Jerry Stanger below him and across from him Metcalfe Spensley and Jack Horn (1925).

114 Sheep washing on Burn Gill, Gouthwaite, Nidderdale, in about 1903. Myers and Willie Atkinson stand in the water. The little girl in white in the centre is Rose Moore.

115 Clipping at Stone House, Dentdale, near the marble works. The group includes Willie Ashburn, Len Burton, and on the right Joseph Allen. The two men sitting facing each other on a sheep stool are castrating a lamb (late 1880s).

Sheep Sales

116 Malham Sheep Fair in the early twentieth century. At this time the farmers sold their own sheep and lambs privately and from year to year had their own pens in the same places. From about 1925 auction sales, which still continue, were run by T. H. Taylor and Son.

117 Clapham Sheep Fair, held the last week in September, prior to 1920 when it finished. Local sales or fairs were general in villages before auction marts took over most of the trade.

118 Settle Sheep Fair, held in the market-place. According to the new market charter of 1708, Settle had two sheep fairs, one on 14 April and the other on 12 October. The change of calendar had moved the spring fair to 26 April, when the market-place was packed with sheep and cattle lined the streets.

119 Hawes Auction Mart on the day of the important shearling tup sales in October 1979. Swaledale shearling tups may sell for from £12,000 to £15,000, and the record is £30,000 in 1986.

Haytime

120 Jim, Albert and John Alderson stop for ten o'clocks whilst mowing with a two-horse Adrian mower at Stone House farm, upper Swaledale. Blossom and Chessie, the horses, were given hay to eat. Rex looks on. John was mowing and Jim *cowling* up, clearing grass away from the mower (late 1930s).

121 Haymakers on a farm in Dentdale turning the hay in haytime (c. 1900).

122 The Dinsdale family of Brown Moor sweeping hay with a Paddy Sweep on Bealer Bank, Hawes (c. 1920).

123 Leading hay on sledges and forking up to the forking hole of a barn on the roadside near Buckden, Wharfdale (1930s).

Modern Haymaking

124 The start of haytime in early July, 1989, on Hoggarth's farm, upper Swaledale. Christopher Calvert is mowing the grass with a disc mower in West Brigg meadow, whilst Raymond Calvert follows on strewing with an acrobat.

125 Baling hay on Lane House Farm, Cold Cotes. Balers enabled hay to be easily transported.

126 Norman Hunter making big bales on Crow Trees farm, upper Swaledale. The big baler drops them off like a hen laying an egg. The bales, seen on the right, were formerly in bags here, but are now wrapped in plastic sheeting.

127 Bruce Bell using a forage harvester taking chopped grass back to a silage clamp on Gill Gate farm, Askrigg, Wensleydale (c. 1983).

Ancillary work

128 Colin Rowling, professional waller from Skipton, walling on Malham Moor in the mild January of 1989. He is employed by farmers needing gaps putting up or walls building.

129 Jim and George Capstick hedging on Hill Top farm, Firbank near Sedbergh, with the river Lune and the Howgill fells in the background (1966).

130 An enclosure wall striking up Rise Hill seen from Dent Town.

131 George and Ralph Scott cutting peat above West Stonesdale, Swaledale, in 1933. Peat cutting was then coming to an end, and it had become usual to use hay spades, not peat spades, to cut out square blocks, which were then sliced in half ready for drying.

132 Leading bracken for bedding in Barbondale off Dentdale (c. 1900).

Shows

133 Young Shorthorn bulls being led at Hawes Agricultural Show in 1906. These events were started there in 1843 when there were classes for Short Horned cattle, half bred, hard and long woolled sheep, fat pigs, dairy produce and for labourers bringing up large families and male and female servants who had lived the longest in one situation. The two shows now in Wensleydale are at Leyburn and Mossdale (Moorcock Show).

134 A familiar sight at any dales show. Here Swaledale hoggs are being judged at Bowes Show in 1965.

135 G. Thompson judging sticks at the
Moorcock Show, upper Wensleydale (1989).

V

· *The Industrial Era* ·

Today the relative quiet of the dales is belied by their industrial past which may be said to have lasted from the early seventeenth to the end of the nineteenth century. Not so long ago intense activity generated local work and traffic. Lead-mines, coal pits, textile mills, knitting, quarries, all using the resources at hand, flourished. They were a part of the general industrial development of northern England. It is on record that half-timers worked in the dales' mills, and that coal leaders or *hurriers*, boys dragging corves of coal by a chain attached to a belt round their waists, worked in the dales' coal pits, just as they did in the mills and coal-mines of the West Riding. As well as being far from concentrations of industry, dales coal never compared with the seams of South Yorkshire and the hard water off limestone was detrimental to the textile industry. Now only the limestone quarries remain, and diverse local employment in industry has ceased.

Lead-mining, with its long heroic story, is the most important. In geo-logical terms lead is found in the Carboniferous system of the Yorkshire dales, so that the mining fields cover a large part of the area. Shallow workings began in Roman times or even earlier with a demand for lead for pipes and roofs, as later the abbeys needed lead for their roofs. Five Roman pigs of lead, three of which have been recorded but lost, have been found in Nidderdale and Swaledale.

Owing to technical improvements, mining took off in the early seventeenth century, promoted by the lords of the manors as owners of the mineral rights. Over the centuries mines and smelt mills appeared everywhere; miles of levels were driven underground, and a new village sprang up at Greenhow. Large companies were formed to advance ambitious projects. Thousands of men were employed in the mines and people from Derbyshire, Cornwall and Ireland flocked to this land of opportunity. The miners were poor, sometimes scholars lacking conventional education. Many lived on smallholdings with a few acres and a cow. Their work was challenging yet unhealthy, a state of affairs mitigated by a lively communal spirit and country sports.

Mining had its effect: woods were felled; hushes spoilt the land; fumes from smelt mill chimneys poisoned cattle until the long surface chimneys were built. Feats of engineering were the miles-long water-courses which fed dams and enlarged tarns, and water, a menace in the mines, drove water wheels to drive pumps and bellows, once to be seen everywhere in the mining fields. Gangs of packhorses carrying wood, ore and pigs of lead, constantly traversed the roads. Another feature were the prolonged and often costly disputes over boundaries beginning in monastic times and culminating in the Beldi Hill trial in Swaledale around 1770 which created bitter factions.

Then at the climax of exploitation the falling price of lead spelled the end about 1880, an end which caused the heartbreaking exodus of families to Lancashire towns and cotton mills, to Leeds and Bradford, to Durham coal fields and emigration to America and the colonies. Small wonder that lead-mining has inspired a proliferation of books, booklets, societies and mine exploration groups.

Coal-mining has received less attention, although coal pits are to be found all over the dales from Wharfedale to Garsdale, and it involved similar hard, often wet, work. Tan Hill pit, where there were several others, closed in 1939. Coal was mined here in the thirteenth century and later warmed the castles of Pendragon and Brough in Cumbria. At Ingleton, pits in use for centuries, closing in 1935, had head stocks not seen elsewhere and a new village for miners. Coal was needed for homes, smelt mills and lime kilns and was transported far and wide by packhorses and donkeys. Following the arrival of the railways, what was then called 'station coal' became easily available and another industry failed.

Here, where all building is in stone, quarries are numerous. They were usually small, supplying material for houses, walls, roads and industrial buildings in their vicinity. Some were township quarries allotted in enclosure awards for the use of the local inhabitants; some specialised in stone roofing slates; some such as Burtersett quarries in Wensleydale and Gilbert Scar in Coverdale were worked by tunnelling into rock. The most important was Scot Gate Ash in Nidderdale whence a fine-grained sandstone was sent all over the country. These too have finished.

What are left now are the huge limestone quarries eating into the hillsides at Swinden near Cracoe, Horton-in-Ribblesdale, near Redmire in Wensleydale, and others. In essence they are a development from the small lime kilns in which up to 100 years ago it was customary procedure for limestone to be burnt for spreading on the land (plate 156). But demand for lime for a multitude of purposes including metalurgical and chemical works and roadstone has necessitated these monsters which cause devastation and heavy traffic but provide work.

One venture is of particular interest. At Stone House marble works in Dentdale an extensive trade developed in sawing and polishing fossilised limestone quarried in the dale for chimney pieces, memorial tablets, staircases, tables and small goods sent all over the country. It was a craft rather than a trade and employed skilled men, and beginning about 1800 it lasted a century. Possibly its heyday was under the partnership of Nixon and Denton, followed by Blackmore and company. Paul Nixon (1765–1850) was a sculptor connected with marble works at Carlisle. He carved busts, and monuments, and supplied chimney pieces for the Council House, Bristol, and for Glyn Mills, bankers, in London.

Lastly there was the attempt at the end of the eighteenth century to draw the dales into the orbit of the Industrial Revolution, then about to transform the textile industries of Lancashire and Yorkshire. It instituted a workforce summoned by mill bells and working set hours. Many cotton mills were started up in the dales by partnerships, often including bankers, who joined together to build mills to contain the new machinery in what seem remote places. Or quite often they adapted disused manorial corn mills to textile mills, using the water wheels for power. Two such cotton mills were at Malham, one near the Cove and the other in Malham itself. Others were at Kettlewell, Linton, Airton and Arncliffe in Littondale, while there was a cluster of mills round Settle in Ribblesdale. Some were burnt down and rebuilt. Most suffered vicissitudes of fortune and changes in use and ownership. One by one they closed down, with a few lingering on into this century. Langcliffe Place near Settle, which was the largest, closed in 1959–60. Many of the buildings can still be seen converted to houses, flats or industrial premises. One little mill, now a ruin near Semerwater, was a silk mill built by William Fothergill of Carr End nearby, probably as a philanthropic venture to provide work.

The wool textile industry suffered similar swings of fortune, but with a difference. It was not new; for hand-loom weaving and hand-knitting had flourished in the dales for centuries. In fact the new mills weaving cloth caused unemployment for handloom weavers. But they also supplied yarn to the hand-knitters and so were mostly built and flourished where the craft of hand-knitting was based in Swaledale, Wensleydale and Dentdale. Tens of thousands of pairs of stockings, exported far and wide by a well organised industry using local wool and importing some of better quality, had been the mainstay. In 1784 Aysgarth, Askrigg and Gayle mills were built for cotton, but soon turned to wool. Round Sedbergh and in Dentdale little woollen mills were built, some of which have gone without trace. Men, women and children knitted and attained a remarkable speed – a skill that has gone. The poorly paid work enabled the industry to survive long after the invention of knitting machines, and it earned extra cash and helped to make a living. Haverdale mill in Swaledale had a short life; about 1903

Hawes mill ceased to work, and Farfield and others near Sedbergh lasted until the 1950s. (Tweeds are still produced at Farfield.) But the textile industry, second only in importance to lead-mining in the dales, had collapsed.

The population of Dentdale, always on a downward trend, fell from 1773 in 1801 to 1076 in 1901. Many people emigrated, and others from Dentdale, Garsdale and Sedbergh moved to Liverpool to run milkhouses – that is, cows were kept in cowsheds off the streets to supply milk. It was a profitable business, and after a time many returned to their native places. As industries failed, the dales were spared further damage to the landscape, but with the general exodus they lost a great deal in human terms.

Hushes

136 Hushes in Gunnerside Gill, Swaledale, looking across the gill. The view shows the devastation caused by this form of lead-mining. Hushes, in which a force of water was released from a dam to reveal lead ore, were a very early form of winning lead.

Lead Mines

137 Old Gang smelt mill, Swaledale, the most impressive remains of lead-mining in the dales, although more ruinous now since this photograph was taken in 1948. The mill was built about 1790 and closed in 1898. On the right can be seen the start of the chimney from the ore hearths climbing up the hillside, and on the top left is the peat house which contained a year's supply of peat and was once thatched.

138 Lane (Loanin) End mine situated on the spit of land where Birkdale beck and Great Sleddale beck join to become the Swale. The building was the engine house for the pumping engine necessary in a mine plagued by water. Old pipes cover a shaft which could be entered via a chamber through the arched opening at the bottom of the photograph. High up in the chamber was a clock. This mine was drowned out (1964).

139 Group of buildings of Cockhill mine, Nidderdale, as seen in 1905. Jackass level and the entrance to Cockhill Adit level are in view.

140 The great Octagon Smelt mill in Arkengarthdale built about 1804 by Easterby Hall and Co. and demolished in 1941. It once had six furnaces, a large water wheel and a long flue ending in a chimney on Crag End (1933).

141 Blacksmith's shop for Beldi Hill lead-mine, Swaledale, in the foreground, and Crackpot Hall beyond (1947).

142 A circular buddle, now gone, on Grassington Moor, with the dressing shed behind it. The buddle was part of the dressing process separating lead ore from the slime by washing (1937).

143 Moss Dams on Ivelet Moor, Swaledale, fed by a long water course and constructed for use in nearby mines. Note the nest of a black-headed gull in the foreground.

Lead Miners

144 A member of the Earby Mines Research Group beside a set of points or 'Turn Rail' in Buckden Gavel mine. The level was driven through limestone and in many places the rails on which the mine tubs ran are still in position.

145 A beautifully arched junction beneath the engine house in the Sir Francis level in Gunnerside Gill. Archers were highly skilled masons. They used two semi-circular iron bars to support planks on which the arch was built. Once constructed, the arch was self-supporting and the framework was removed from beneath.

146 Thomas Blackah, lead-miner and dialect poet (1826–95). He worked in the mines at Greenhow, taking bargains in partnerships, and at one stage he emigrated to America but returned. He compiled almanacs and wrote some delightful dialect poems. The mines closed towards the end of his life and he died in Leeds. (H. L. Bruff.)

147 Thomas Hall of West Burton, retired lead-miner in his seventies. He was a Derbyshire man who came to Yorkshire in 1887, where he worked first at Keld Head mine, then Braithwaite, both in Wensleydale. He also worked at Petticoat flot, a mine in Walden, and at Gammersgill in Coverdale (1905).

148 Kit Peacock of Redmire, Wensleydale, retired lead-miner who had worked at Keld Head mine, near Wensley. He lived at Lightfoot Hall, Redmire, and was naturally studious (early 1930s).

Coal Pits

149 The New Ingleton Colliery in 1914. It was distinguished by its head stocks and was closed in 1935.

150 Tan Hill coal pit, one of several pits worked for centuries on the high lands between upper Swaledale and Stainmore. Although the coal was not good, it was in great demand over a wide area, and in the autumn, men, horses and carts coming from far and wide queued for fuel for winter. The pit closed a few years after this photograph was taken (1933).

Marble and Pottery

151 Stone House marble works, Dentdale, below Arten Gill viaduct on the Settle–Carlisle line. The two mills where the marble was sawn and polished and the showroom were closed owing to a dispute in 1908.

152 Draughts board made by workmen in their spare time at the marble works. Set on cast-iron legs, they were popular for public houses.

153 Pottery cow and calf now in Dentdale, was in the 1860s over the fanlight of a doorway of a milk house in Vine Street, Liverpool. Milk poured in at the back of the head came out at the teats.

Copper

154 Disused copper mine in Great Sleddale, off upper Swaledale. Little is known about it except that three men who worked there lodged at Stone House nearby about 1900 (1964).

Quarries and Limestone

155 Workmen at Seavy Quarry, Burtersett, c. 1895. There were several quarries round this village near Hawes. The industry was given impetus by the arrival of the railway in 1878; it peaked about 1890 and gradually declined until it ceased in 1931. Thousands of tons of stone were despatched from Hawes station, some of it to Lancashire to build the expanding cotton towns.

156 Lime kiln on the lane above Carperby, Wensleydale. There used to be two here, one a township kiln which has gone and this one, which belonged to the Bolton Estates. They are to be seen all over the dales in various states of repair, and were used for burning limestone to spread on the land, a practice which was often specified in leases of land and which ceased during the last century.

157 Horton Quarry, Ribblesdale, seen from the top of Penyghent. One of several quarries in
Ribblesdale, it was started in 1887 by John Delaney, whose firm became Settle Limes in 1939,

then I.C.I. and is now Tarmac. Chiefly refractory material, dust for brick-making and roadstone is supplied (1984).

Reservoir

158 Group at the wedding of John Wilfred Haines and Alice Annie Cox at the canteen at Scar House, upper Nidderdale, in 1925. John Haines was an engine and crane driver, and was known as 'Young London' to distinguish him from his father 'London Jack', who had worked on the building of the London Underground.

159 Building the dam at Scar House Reservoir, Nidderdale, in October 1925, the third reservoir to be built in Nidderdale for Bradford Corporation Waterworks. It was started in 1920 and completed in 1936. Approximately 1000 people lived there in village hostels with all amenities, and the Nidd Valley Light Railway was extended to serve it.

Cornmill

160 Hawes water corn mill below the bridge on Gayle beck. The Chapmans were the last millers and Edward Chapman started the Wensleydale Dairy for the making of Wensleydale cheese. The water wheel has gone, but its supports remain (c. 1900).

Textiles

161 The former cotton mill at Airton on the river Aire, built about 1834 by Isaac and John Dewhurst on the site on a corn mill belonging to Bolton Priory. It closed in 1909 when the Dewhursts moved to Skipton and after several uses is now residential flats.

162 Past employees of Airton mill; a photograph taken when the mill closed in 1909. A second photograph shows forty employees of that date.

163 Gayle Mill near Hawes, built in 1784 used in turn for cotton, flax and wool. By 1867 it was a saw mill. It contains a turbine said to be the oldest in Europe.

164 Hebblethwaite Hall woollen mill the forerunner of Farfield mill, both near Sedbergh. It was built about 1792 by Robert Foster, and was later run by Joseph Dover who in 1837 built Farfield mill. Here yarn was spun for cloth and for knitting. Hebblethwaite became a bobbin and saw mill, and later fell into ruin.

165 Yore mill, Aysgarth, Wensleydale, situated on the river Ure, close to the bridge, built as a cotton mill in 1784, in ruin in 1818, burnt down in 1852 and rebuilt as we see it today in the photograph. It became a woollen mill spinning yarn for knitting, a corn mill, and is now a carriage museum (c. 1900).

166 Haverdale Mill, Low Row, Swaledale. The large four-storied mill with an attic was built by the Knowleses, worsted spinners and hosiery manufacturers, about 1835. Yarn was spun for knitting and in 1840 carpet looms were installed. In spite of the introduction of steam power, the enterprise foundered about 1870. The mill was finally pulled down in the 1930s.

167 Dee mill remembered as Hud's Foss Brewery near Cowgill, Dentdale. It was originally built as a woollen mill by Dawson Bannister described in 1822 as a worsted and yarn stocking manufacturer. It was demolished over 100 years ago and the stone used to build Ewegales farmhouse. There was a bridge here across the river Dee.

Handknitters

168 (*Below*) Mary Kirkbride (1830–1922), known as Molly i' t'Wynd, outside her home at Gayle near Hawes. She was a famous knitter who knitted bump stockings for sailors and jackets for the Smiths of Hawes mill and later for a firm in Kendal and the Dovers of Farfield mill, who sent carriers' carts to Hawes (1890s).

169 (*Right*) A Dent knitter, Polly Stephenson, who has her *clue* (ball of wool) hanging from her belt so that she can knit and walk about. The flexed position of her hands is typical. In the inset she is bringing home cops of yarn delivered at Dent Town from Kendal in the 1880s (1930s).

170 (*Left*) Mary Allen of Dent (1857–1924), knitter of patterned gloves. These are to be seen together with her knitting stick and needles at the Dales Countryside Museum at Hawes, Wensleydale. Her mother knitted gloves for Queen Victoria, with a crown on the palm, and also for Lord Palmerston.

171 Two Dent knitters at the turn of the century. Although knitting sheaths are hidden by their arms, they were no doubt using them, and a stocking made of bump (coarse wool) lies across one knitter's lap. Note the position of the hands close to the tips of the needles. 'Keep short needles', they used to say.

172 A group of dales' knitters who knit in
their homes for the firm of Swaledale
Woollens, gathered together at Muker in
1989. David Morris, holding the Swaledale
ram, founded the firm with his wife in 1974.
Swaledale Woollens has a shop in Muker
and carries on the tradition of hand-knitting
in the dales.

VI

· Occupations · Shops · Inns ·

The preceding pages did not include the professions, the craftsmen, women's and other occupations. Thomas Dunham Whitaker, historian (1759–1821), and Adam Sedgwick, the geologist (1785–1873), are two of the most famous dalesmen in the immediate past; the one compiled classic histories of Craven and Richmondshire and the other left a unique description of Dentdale. Many luminaries are doctors: George Birkbeck of Settle, who founded Mechanics Institutes, also William Hillary of Wensleydale, John Fothergill of Raydale, John Haygarth of Garsdale, and Robert Willan of Sedbergh, who respectively pioneered work on tropical diseases, diphtheria, isolation of fevers and dermatology. In the twentieth century Will Pickles (1885–1969), who joined a practice at Aysgarth in 1912, has carried on the torch by his work on infectious diseases (plate 173).

The arts are represented, but mostly by people who have come to the dales from elsewhere. Jessie Fothergill (fl. 1899) and May Bradley of Carperby were minor novelists of local origin. Better known are Halliwell Sutcliffe and C. J. Cutcliffe Hyne linked with Wharfedale; Dorothy Una Ratcliffe and George Jackson with Wensleydale, and Thomas Armstrong who based one of his novels on Swaledale. Amongst artists, Reginald Smith and Fred Lawson were water colourists. It would be invidious and too long a list to single out all the present-day writers and artists who have adopted the dales for their inspiration. Also it is a phenomenon that during the last ten or so years many artists and potters have settled there. The dales too have their own magazine, *The Dalesman*, which has just celebrated fifty years of publication.

Formerly the basic complement of craftsmen in a market-town was a cabinet-maker, a miller, a saddler, a printer, a tinsmith, a rope-maker, a tanner, several joiners, masons, tailors, blacksmiths and shoemakers. Today, because of the scale of mass production, there only remain the printers, the masons, joiners, the rare blacksmith and the still more rare rope-maker, such as one firm which flourishes at Hawes. The blacksmith has turned into a plumber and central heating engineer. Printers are often long established, for example Lamberts of Settle (plate 177) and the Wensleydale Press at Hawes, which traces its origins back to the 1840s. Joiners and masons are the survivors, nowadays working non-stop to restore derelict houses or to alter premises for shops and cafés. In the spring especially, hammering is the theme sound of the dales.

Women's lives have been transformed as elsewhere by birth control, and electricity for lighting, washing and cooking. No more families of teens of children, no more butter or cheese-making, which has gone to the dairies, or the scrubbing and sanding of kitchen floors, or the black leading of kitchen ranges. Instead there is abundant part- or full-time work nowadays augmented by the tourist industry.

Fifty years ago there were many more little shops kept by both men and women often selling goods from a front room. Shops come and go, and over the years change ownership and the goods sold. Since farmers' wives ceased to make butter and cheese to barter for groceries and clothes, the traditionally combined grocer-cum-draper has mostly gone. Ironmongers too in this era of gadgets, plastic and electricity have changed their character. We picture two which had foundries – Manbys at Skipton and Todds at Summerbridge, Nidderdale – and we have been shown the catalogue dated about 1830 of R. Spence & Co.,

Market Place, Richmond, in which the items read like the inventory of a museum. A few are: Jews' harps, sugar nippers and crushers, powder flasks, stomach and feet warmers, and American floating washing machines. Wages were low. When Ronald Gilling, who worked at Spence's for fifty years, started in 1903 he earned 5s. a week for a twelve-hour day.

Old-established shops sometimes have clockwork toys to decorate windows at Christmas. A Santa Claus on a sledge pulled by reindeer still appears in Mason's shop window at Hawes, and at Sedbergh a monkey up a stick with a nodding head pretending to eat an apple used to come out at Christmas. It was bought by Miss Sedgwick's father who once a week walked to Low Gill station to go to buy goods in Manchester. Similarly the Blythes of Hawes travelled by coach to London and brought back books, shoes and bonnets. Before headgear was mostly abandoned, milliners and straw-hat makers were usual.

At the present day the village shop, often combined with the village post office, has to compete with small and large supermarkets in the neighbouring market towns. On the other hand, influenced by tourism, craft and gift shops spring up – one at Kettlewell occupies the old blacksmith's shop – and disused premises and barns are converted into new knitwear and outdoor clothing establishments.

Like shops, many inns have gone over the years – in 1822 Askrigg had four, now only two. There were once the Anglers Arms at Kilnsey, the Bull's Head near

Cracoe, inns at Gearstones and Newby Head on the Richmond to Lancaster turnpike and many more. At the same time, taking advantage of the tourist boom new ones and also guest houses have opened up. Some inns are famous, some historic, some for fishermen, some very popular, and one, the Devonshire Arms at Bolton Abbey, has gone upmarket. Prices today are very different from 7s. for bed and breakfast in the 1930s and the shilling dinners for the carriers and farmers at the inns in market towns. 'Wrapped up like a shilling dinner' used to be a saying.

173 William Norman Pickles CBE, MD (1885–1969) with his wife, Gertrude, and daughter, Patience, outside their home at Aysgarth, Wensleydale. He became the most famous GP in the country for his work on infectious diseases, published *Epidemiology in Country Practice*, was the first president of the new college of general practitioners and was loved and respected by his patients.

Authors

174 John Charles Cutcliffe Hyne (1866–1944), with his wife on the left, his daughter, Nancy, next to him and friends on the bridge at Kettlewell. His father, a vicar, moved to Bradford when the boy was three, and spent holidays at Kettlewell where in 1901 they bought a house. Educated at Clare College, he became a great traveller and began writing adventure stories for boys. He contributed to many magazines, and wrote numerous books, many featuring the popular character, Captain Kettle (1911).

175 Marie Hartley and Joan Ingilby, writers of books on Yorkshire and the dales, in their garden at Askrigg, Wensleydale. Marie Hartley has illustrated all the books with either woodcuts, line drawings or photographs. They have lived here for over forty years and between them have written and had published twenty-one books (1989).

Parson and Printer

176 The Rev. Robert Pickering, vicar of Cowgill, Dentdale, who was a bachelor, with his niece, in a photograph taken at the vicarage. He was a photographer and took many of the Dentdale photographs in this book (c. 1900).

177 The offset litho printing room of J. W. Lambert and Sons, Settle, printers, stationers and booksellers. The firm has been in operation since 1881, and the present owner, John Lambert, is the fourth generation. In the late 1960s they changed to offset printing and in 1974/5 started photo-setting and colour printing. Many small books are printed here (1989).

Gamekeeper and Postman

178 William Marwood with his spaniels, Topsy and Taffy. He was gamekeeper on the Scargill estate, south of Barnard Castle, from 1940 to 1972. His territory was chiefly grouse moor, a circuit of seventeen miles, with some lower ground. He says 'A gamekeeper is always quiet. He feels with his feet' (1966).

179 John Cowan (1908–89) of Halton Gill, Littondale, delivering letters to Mrs Dolphin at Cosh about 1928. The post came by wagonette from Grassington to Halton Gill about 11.30 am, and John took letters three days a week to Cosh and three to Penyghent. It took him an hour to Cosh and rather longer to Penyghent, and he was paid 12s. a week.

Craftsmen

180 The joiner's shop at the top end of Middlesmoor, Nidderdale, run by the Lee family for some 150 years until 1982. In 1830 Richard Lee was a coal miner and carpenter. The firm continues as Lee and Holmes, but no one in it is in the direct line (1890s).

181 George (blacksmith) and Donald Wood at Bolton Abbey, with hand-made iron door furniture including bolts, handles, door bands, crooks and hand-made nails, for the church of St John the Baptist at Pinner, Middlesex. Donald kept the books and organised their taxi and garage business. The blacksmith's shop has been a café since 1971 (1954).

182 Andrew Hague, potter, came to Askrigg in Wensleydale in 1975/6, and is now established at Old School House, where he operates a large oil-fired kiln firing both stoneware and porcelain. Collections of his work are to be found all over the country and Europe. His wife makes decorative troughs.

183 Alf Allinson, cobbler, at Horton-in-Ribblesdale. A photograph taken by James A. Rawcliffe, vicar of Horton 1924–41 (c. 1930s).

184 Robert Burrow (1878–1953), saddler at Hawes repairing a saddle (1947).

Road Men

185 Alf Burnett, lengthman in Coverdale, probably between Caldbergh and Coverham church (1932).

186 Council workmen relaying cobbles in the main street of Dent Town opposite the fountain. The streets of the then market towns such as Dent and Askrigg were paved with cobbles in the eighteenth century, and a paviour who laid cobbles round houses or in cowsheds or in the streets and in market places was a recognised occupation (1960s).

Masons and Railway Men

187 Neville Thwaite, John Percival, masons and helpers replacing a barn roof at Moor Road, Askrigg.

188 The staff of eighteen men at Hawes station in the early twentieth century. In 1881 there were twenty-one men employed based at Hawes. The poster on the right extols the Settle–Carlisle route to Scotland. The Wensleydale line closed in 1954.

Women's Work

189 Agnes Metcalfe with her geese at Appersett, Wensleydale. In past times the rearing and sale of geese was an additional source of income especially for women.

190 Lily Simpson making a round pound of butter by rolling it sideways on the board at Westfield, Nidderdale (1965).

191 Margaret Ethel Willis binding Wensleydale cheeses at the Manor House dairy, Carperby. Cheese-making started here when the Willises ceased to keep Beef Shorthorns and changed over to Dairy Shorthorns. Manor House won several championships at the London Dairy Show and sent cheese to Fortnum and Mason (c. 1898).

192 Chris Alderson assisted with clipping sheep by his daughters, Eleanor and Jennifer, at Black Howe farm, upper Swaledale (1965). If there are no sons, daughters help in many ways on the farm, equally wives help husbands. Women are depicted clipping sheep in the Luttrell Psalter.

193 Mary Amelia Alderson (1912–89) at Black Howe farm, upper Swaledale, cleaning matting – a very popular floor covering. She had two daughters and lived with her husband, Christopher, at Black Howe for twenty-nine years before semi-retirement to Keld, retiring in 1976 to Richmond.

194 Elizabeth (Lizzie) Percival (1900–77) mixing the batter for a Yorkshire pudding at Old School House, Askrigg (1965).

195 Nellie Raw hanging out the washing at Lane Farm, Muker, Swaledale (1989).

Volunteers

196 Three members of the 12th North Yorkshire Rifle Volunteers formed in 1859 – William Thomas Shields, Jack Hunter and Tom Batty of Redmire. The old Loyal Dales Volunteers, who started during the Napoleonic Wars, had been disbanded, but distrust of France gave rise to numerous rifle volunteer corps. They were the forerunners of the Territorial Army and the Home Guard of the Second World War. Here they practised target shooting at Ellerans above Castle Bolton and used a moving target of a running deer on the scar (1890s).

197 The Monkey Bridge, near Redmire, is the second of two bridges leading from Redmire to West Witton, both washed away in floods. The first had iron spikes on a post as a means of access, hence its name. They enabled the rifle volunteers to cross the river from West Witton to the Drill Hall at Redmire built in 1862 by Captain Christopher Other of Elm House. The hall is now the village shop (1884).

Shops

198 Travelling van for the sale of agricultural equipment. George Robinson, centre with his hand on the door, and customers, H. Jackson in the van, at Hawes Auction Mart. He visited Hawes, Bentham, Gisburn and Clitheroe markets, as his nephew still does in 1989 (1966).

199 Fred Manby and Bro., ironmonger's shop at a corner of the High Street, Skipton, which was established in 1816–17 and closed in 1985. Manbys' were iron founders, wholesale ironmongers and agricultural implement makers. Their foundry, Craven Iron Works, off the Keighley Road, once made fireplaces embossed with their name.

200 Todd Bros, ironmongers, opposite the school at Summerbridge, Nidderdale. Behind the shop was the Nidd Valley Foundry started by Joseph Todd and William Gill about 1861, which about 1890 employed some twenty men. They manufactured machinery, implements and fireplaces. The foundry fell into ruin and the shop has gone (1910).

201 Robson Wood, department store, Finkle Street, Richmond, was started in 1820 by Robson and Wood, and although it changed hands several times, it retained its original name to the end. It closed in March 1984. The firm toured the dales selling goods, and young men served their apprenticeship there (1905–10).

202 Market day at Hawes in the early years of the last century. The shops were rebuilt about 1900. Both Fosters on the left and Moores on the right were grocers and drapers. Fosters display bedding on a bed on the pavement. Moores became Metcalfes, grocers, and is now an outdoor clothing shop, whilst Fosters became Elijah Allen, who moved from Gayle in 1930.

203 Village shop at Clapham (still there) which sold groceries and haberdashery, owned by Mrs Brown (in the doorway) helped by four daughters and her son Johnny (on the left holding his boater.) On Saturdays Johnny sold goods by horse and cart from Clapham to Horton-in-Ribblesdale (1920s).

204 William Lord, grocer at Austwick. He also brought coal and goods by horse and cart from Clapham station. The cart is decorated for a gala (early twentieth century).

205 Dee Cottage, Cowgill, Dentdale, a shop which sold everything kept by Richard and Ellen Jane Bayne. Formerly a milliner's, the shop was opened before the First World War. Richard was a joiner who was followed by his son-in-law. On the left is the pot shop whose windows came from Dent Methodist chapel. The shop closed in 1980 (1908).

206 A grocer's and draper's shop in the market-place at Muker, kept by the Raws for over 100 years, beginning in different premises. Christopher Raw, shopkeeper in 1890, was the grandfather of the last, Jenny Raw, who retired and closed the shop in 1974 (1938).

207 Post Office and village shop at Lofthouse, Nidderdale. The owner, Beatrice Godley, who came from Weardale to Nidderdale, attends to a customer, Eli Harrison, retired shepherd, who worked for four farmers on Stean Moor until about 1980.

208 Roger and Cynthia Parry serving customers at the village shop and Post Office, Kettlewell, Wharfedale.

209 Jim Nelson, shoemaker, Settle, whose great-great-grandfather moved to Settle from Cononley near Keighley in 1847 and prospered supplying boots to the navvies making the railway. Jim's father was the last to make shoes and his son, Daniel, is the fifth generation. He is demonstrating the saying 'A shoemaker looks with his fingers'.

210 Kit Calvert buys a stick from Agnes Blythe at the Post Office at Hawes (late 1920s).

Inns

211 A group outside the Flying Horse Shoe Hotel near the station at Clapham. The winged horseshoe depicts the crest of the Farrers, lords of the manor of Clapham, who built the hotel in 1850, following the arrival of the railway at Clapham in July 1849. The proprietor, Henry Coates, may be second man left in the second row (1890s).

212 The Tennant Arms at Kilnsey, Wharfedale, takes its name from the Tennant family, long resident at Chapel House nearby. In 1822 H. Trueman was the innkeeper (late 1920s).

213 The Cathole Inn, Keld, then kept by William Hutchinson, was closed in 1954. The old inn building, originally called the Miners Arms, is still there below it (1930s).

214 Decorated horse-drawn carts drawn up in front of the Crown Hotel, Middlesmoor, Nidderdale. Probably the event was the coronation of Edward VII. The innkeeper was then J. T. Carling, and his daughter, Katie, is looking out of the window. In 1822 William Driver was the landlord of the Crown.

215 Tan Hill Inn, 1732 feet above sea level, the highest inn in England on the borders of North Yorkshire and Durham. It owes its existence to several coal pits worked here since medieval times. The building on the left has been demolished and the inn itself, of eighteenth-century date, altered. Susan Peacock, landlady from 1903 to 1937, was famous (1960).

VII

· *Transport* · *Recreation* ·

In the 1840s the industrialised dales, served by horse transport, attracted plans for ambitious routes for railways, most of which never materialised. But branch lines were built to Richmond in 1846, to Leyburn in 1856, on to Hawes in 1878, to Pateley Bridge in 1862 and to Grassington in 1902. Skirting the southern edge of the dales is the early main line from Leeds to Morecambe on which Clapham station was formerly a junction for a line through Ingleton to Low Gill. Traversing the Pennines in the north, the Settle to Carlisle opened in 1876, linked with a branch line to Hawes. All except the two main lines have been closed or truncated, that to Grassington for passengers in 1930, to Nidderdale in 1936, to Hawes in 1954, to Low Gill in 1966 and to Richmond in 1969.

At the time the branch lines made a strong impact. Catterick Camp station on the Richmond branch was important in two world wars, and the Nidd Valley line was extended to Scar House when the reservoir was being built (plate 217). Quarries despatched stone, farmers

milk, tourism was boosted. The brass band festival at Hardraw Scar owed its origin to the arrival of the railway at Hawes, and trains brought trippers to Bolton Abbey in the early years of the century. One feels that commercialisation of the dales began with the railways, especially in Wensleydale where the line ran from end to end. Yet we regret their passing and marvel how goods were sent so speedily by train.

The Settle to Carlisle line was chosen as the Midland Company's route to Scotland, and with its cuttings, tunnels and viaducts it has been described as 'the crowning glory of British railroad genius'. We remember it with the Thames-Clyde express rushing through, freight trains carrying anything from lime to motor cars, and the stations with station masters and staff the hubs of life along the line. Recently, for ten years British Rail threatened closure, and a large body of rail enthusiasts rallied to its defence. Success came in 1989, and this historic line, a national monument, was reprieved.

The railways sealed the doom of the coaching era just as the petrol engine has finished branch lines and horse traffic. Statistics reveal that in 1905 there were 16,000 motor cars in the UK, and in 1978 14,069,000. Forty years ago second-hand cars were usual here, and women seldom drove. Now the reverse is the rule. Gradually the dales have been discovered and invaded by ever increasing traffic, especially in the last ten years, added to by coaches bringing groups from all over the country and America. It has meant prosperity for those engaged in tourism, but in summer is often beyond the capacity of village streets. On the other hand, coaches take parties from the dales on outings, and as seen on plates 228–31 modern vehicles have brought welcome amenities.

Sport might be said to have begun with stag hunting in the forests and the great chases over the hills; for this is sporting country for hunting, fishing, shooting and racing. Both Richmond and Middleham held race meetings organised by the gentry dating back to the sixteenth century, and Middleham still has renowned racing stables. In 1793 there were Reeth Bridge races, and in the 1840s Hurst races for horses owned by miners, ore and lead carriers.

Packs of hounds and beagles kept all over the dales have a long history, and the dales rivers offer trout fishing, a specialised subject in itself. As for grouse shooting on the moors, it has turned into big business. At the turn of the century a Wensleydale sportsman wrote that grouse shooting 'claims a premier place amongst contemporary sports' for the enjoyment of 'health giving breezes', 'the delicious odour of purple heather' and 'the wild romantic scenery'.

What strikes us about the age-old entertainments of former times is the whole-hearted enjoyment of them. Feasts, fairs, sports and the later chapel anniversaries and Sunday School outings were part of life savoured to the full and looked forward to from year to year. Feasts, derived from saints' days and religious festivals, lasted a few days or a week and were times for reunions, for weddings and celebrating. Formerly there were dog trails, donkey races, climbing the greasy pole, eating penny buns soaked in treacle, and grinning through *barfams* (horse collars). Quoits, wallops and foot races for all age groups were and are traditional, and the prizes of copper kettles were won and displayed with pride. Now the fell race is the highlight of sports, once for local competitors but now attracting a large field. There were stalls for clothes, pottery and sweetmeats, and children were given fairings. Food always was and is important. People saved up to buy huge joints of beef. At Askrigg October fair it is remembered that one household cooked forty-five pounds of beef, also ham and tongue, and sat down thirty at table and when they had finished another lot came.

Changing in form over the years, dancing was the foremost recreation. In remote dales the Kissing and Cushion dances continued from distant times, and folk dances with specific tunes, such as Buttered Peas, Turn Off Six, Huntsman's Chorus, were collected in 1931, mostly in upper Wharfedale. In the last century some villages had dancing masters, and polkas, quadrilles, lancers and waltzes prevailed, all adapted from folk dances. There were Conservative and Liberal Balls with Sir Roger de Coverley. Many events ended in dances to tunes played on the fiddle or concertina in the long rooms of the inns. For these men put on a clean *kytle* (cotton coat) and carried their shoes as they walked miles over the moors to them in their clogs.

Music is the traditional art, ranging from singing to brass bands. Formerly almost every village had its band, which at Christmas time toured the surrounding neighbourhood. We read of the Askrigg Singers and the Gunnerside Choir in the 1840s, and in the 1930s the Swaledale Veterans and later the Keld Singers who broadcast on radio, famous for their sweet voices and the rendering of 'Beautiful Swaledale'. Operatic societies and choirs led by dedicated conductors staged ambitious productions and elaborate pantomimes. An operatic society was formed at Settle in 1879, the Wensleydale Tournament of Song was begun in 1898 and the Wharfedale Musical Festival in 1907. With these go dramatic societies and the famous Georgian theatre at Richmond opened in 1788, rediscovered in this century, and offering both music and drama. Ingleton is fortunate in having a fine Community Centre opened in 1974, and used for concerts, lectures and exhibitions.

Societies from the old established clubs to the many present-day groups cover every activity. Once there were numerous Friendly Societies for mutual insurance, now only a few. Women's Institutes started in 1915, soon spread, and have given women a national voice. Undoubtedly newcomers have pioneered and boosted a range of societies – local history, botany, the arts, spinning, conservation and other subjects. Above all, walking draws people to the hills; caving and pot-holing attract the explorers, and the new sport of hang-gliding the adventurous. Museums at Richmond, Reeth, Hawes, Grassington, Skipton and Settle keep alive memories of the continuous history of the dales from those early ages to the present day.

From time to time throughout the introductions in this book we have described present-day trends in the Yorkshire Dales: modern farming methods, the dilution of dales' character, and the escalation of tourism. The latter, generating traffic and over-crowding in places, has partially taken the place of the former industries. In addition, newcomers retiring to live here or buying second homes, causing inflated prices for houses, has increased during the last ten or fifteen years. The general appearance of the dales remains largely unspoilt thanks to the planning policies of the Yorkshire Dales National Park, and as we move into the next century, there will be consolidation but more change, especially in farming, seems inevitable.

Railways

216 The last train on the Wensleydale line at Askrigg station on 24 April 1954. The porter, A. Lomax, is about to hand over the tablet to the engine driver. After the signalman had accepted the train, the tablet was released from a machine at the station and handed over to allow the train to proceed. This system was used on single track lines.

217 A goods train carrying cement to Scar House, upper Nidderdale, on the Nidd Valley Light Railway when the reservoir for Bradford Corporation was being built. For this heavy load it took three engines to pull up to Scar, and the train has just emerged from a tunnel. Harry Gray is on the first engine (1920s).

218 Freight train passing through Dent station in the days when the Settle–Carlisle line was an important freight route between England and Scotland. The train in the distance was removing redundant material following the closure of many intermediate stations to goods and passenger traffic (1974).

219 (*Overleaf*) The veteran steam locomotive, Green Arrow, crossing Dent Head Viaduct on the Settle–Carlisle line for a special event on 13 May 1989. The famous Settle–Carlisle line, under threat of closure for six years, was reprieved in 1989. Many people and many organisations have worked hard to save it.

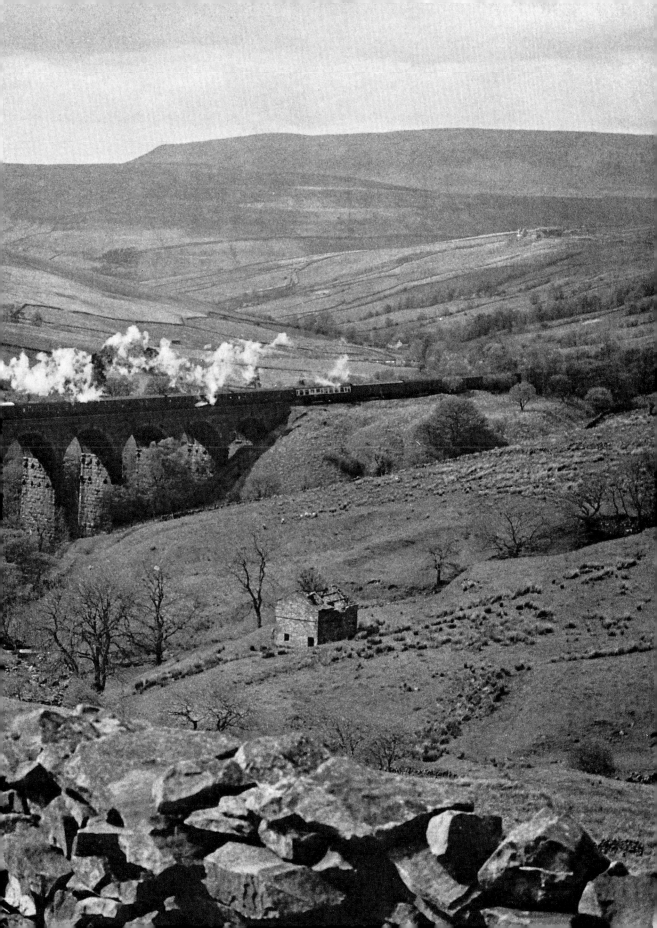

220 Three fully trained signalwomen – Annie Sunter, Winnie Sunter and Edith Sedgwick – manned the Selside signal box on the Settle–Carlisle line in the Second World War. They each had one full day off in three weeks. The line was very busy all the time with freight, passenger and often troop trains (March 1945).

221 Snow plough at Ribblehead station on the Settle–Carlisle line in the late nineteenth century. In February 1933 it was closed for nearly a week and in 1947 it was closed in places for two months and elsewhere acted as a lifeline for food. (Houghton and Foster.)

Outings

222 Robert Wood with his horse, Dick, and wagonette in the yard of the old blacksmith's shop at Bolton Abbey. Fourteen vehicles used to ply between Bolton Abbey station, the Hole in the Wall, the Cavendish Pavilion and the Strid. Robert is driving the last wagonette. All of them finished in the early 1940s.

223 Outing to Bolton Castle, Wensleydale, by horse and trap. The passengers are most likely William Calvert (blacksmith and innkeeper) and his wife from Askrigg, and the piebald horse is 'Old Bowly' (early twentieth century).

Motor Vehicles

224 Family outing from Wetherby to the dales stopping for a picnic at Ribblehead. *From left to right*: Gertrude Hartley (author's mother), Ella Pontefract (*just seen*), her mother, Emma Pontefract and her father, John Pontefract. The motor-car is a Riley special touring model. It was black with red leather upholstery. Note the smoke of a train on the Settle–Carlisle line (1929).

225 An interesting old motor-car. It was built about 1920, and had a Ford engine, a Bosch magneto, a Zenith carburettor and an English body. The magneto came from a German 'plane shot down in the First World War. T. W. Ellison is in the driving seat, Bertha Ellison behind with George the small boy in Dentdale (1922).

226 William Beck (1870–1942), who owned the first motor bike in Malhamdale. He came to Airton at the age of eleven from Hebden, and was apprenticed to his father, who was estate joiner at Scosthrop House (c. 1912).

227 Taxi at Bainbridge, Wensleydale, in 1927. Sitting in it are Olive Bedford (née Holliday), Marie Hartley and Eva Johnson, who were on a walking tour beginning at Richmond and ending in Wharfedale. The usual fourth member of the party, Ella Pontefract, was on this occasion unable to come. The taxi is a Maudslay c. 1912, but it was probably rebodied in the 1920s.

Modern Services

228 Refuse collection at Barden Tower, Wharfedale. What would Lady Anne Clifford have thought of it? It is a boon in modern times, eliminating ash tips from coal fires down river and beck sides, as well as old bedsteads filling up gaps in walls (1989).

229 Milk tanker at Middleham taking milk from G. F. W. Walton and Sons, Park House Farm, Middleham, to the Milk Marketing Board Dairy at Northallerton (1989).

230 The librarian, Geoff Atkinson, and Mary Ellison at Greenwell, Dentdale, with the Cumbria County library van which calls every three weeks. A blackbird had recently made its nest and laid eggs under the front wing, but . eventually it took fright and flew off at Arnside.

231 Dales bus waiting to go up Swaledale in Richmond market-place.

Fell Race

232 The Fell Race at Burnsall Feast Sports in 1936. It has been run here for over 100 years. The small number of competitors, all local men shown here in the photograph, contrasts with the average number of 150 to 200 who come from all over to compete now. Sports in the dales now include a fell race.

Sports

233 Walkers on the Pennine Way on Cam Fell with Ingleborough in the background.

234 (*Overleaf*) Mountain bikes on Fremington Edge, with Calver Hill behind and a glimpse of Reeth Lane. The group is led by Steve Chapman, who owns the bikes and organises small parties of riders. The sport has existed about seven years, but only recently become popular locally. The bikes each have some twenty gears, are very expensive, and have to keep to certain regulations.

235 A grouse shooting party on the Ingleborough estate, probably near Gearstones.

236 One of the oldest photographs of caving in Yorkshire. It shows Mr Parsons and Miss Booth at the telephone at the bottom of Gaping Gill at Whitsuntide 1906. There is a Booth and Parsons crawl down Gaping Gill. In the 1920s and 1930s Miss Booth was an intrepid traveller. She had crossed the Gobi desert, had been attacked by pirates and had other adventures. (J. Telford.)

237 Jim (Sproats) Blades, for many years the Hawes postman and a famous fisherman with his grandson, also Jim Blades known as Pinky (c. 1930). Pinky got his first licence in 1932 at the age of seven, and still fishes when he has time.

238 A motor car in difficulties on Park Rash between Kettlewell and Coverdale competing in the Whit Monday Endurance Race between London and Newcastle. The Wisemans from Kettlewell took up horses and chains to help competitors up this notorious hill then unmade (1920s).

239 The Richmond Meet, the most important event in the calendar at Richmond, outside the King's Head Hotel in the market-place in 1893. A cyclists' meet, it was started the year before, and has continued annually ever since, except in war-time, on the May Bank Holiday weekend. Recently the event has included a cycle race round the town.

240 Hang-glider flying out from Wether Fell, upper Wensleydale, towards Duerley Bottom. The hillside opposite is Dodd Fell. The dales are ideal for this sport, which started here in 1973 and soon became popular.

Children's Sports

241 Children and some grown-ups in fancy dress at Askrigg Sports about 1950. Village annual sports days in the dales always include fancy dress, often wonderfully inventive and topical.

242 Boys' pillow fight at the children's sports at Carlton, Coverdale, in June 1965.

243 November the fifth bonfire and children with fireworks at Askrigg, 1960s.

244 Leslie, Karen and Richard Allen and a friend inspecting a catch of crayfish on the banks of the river Ure at Abbey Heads, Askrigg (1965).

Societies

245 Richmond Theatre Royal (1940). The scene is at the back of the pit below the Shakespeare box as at that date the main stage was not ready for use. It is posed by members of the Richmond Amateur Dramatic Society rehearsing *Twelfth Night*. The theatre was built in 1788, and is one of the oldest and best-preserved Georgian theatres in England. (Southern.)

246 (*Opposite below*) The cast of Hawes Operatic Society for their first performance, which was *The Pirates of Penzance*, staged in April 1925.

247 Malham Women's Institute celebrating the twenty-first anniversary of their formation. Mrs A. R. Foster is the president (1950).

248 The Swaledale singers, an augmented group, giving a concert at Aysgarth in the 1930s. From left to right: Dick Guy, A. E. Wright, Laurie Rukin, Chris Alderson, Mary Clarkson (Peacock), John Peacock (brim of hat), Richard Alderson, Ernest Alderson and Gladys Guy (pianist).

Events

249 Botanising in Grass Wood in August 1909. The wood near Grassington harboured the deer in the Middle Ages, and in more recent times has become botanically famous. It and the many archaeological features near Grassington has inspired the Upper Wharfedale Field Society, formed in 1949, and its six sections.

250 Spinners at an event at Clapham. *From left to right*: Val Marshall, Glenys Colton, Jessica Hart. Groups of spinners and weavers, making use of local wool (fleeces), have for some time flourished in several dales (1989).

251 Buckden Feast in 1966. The bandsmen are having a rest and onlookers gather round a childrens' roundabout. Annual feast days were great reunions for families separated by economic circumstances.

252 Grassington Feast held in October.

Festivities

253 Festivities of Middlesmoor and Lofthouse, Nidderdale, for the coronation of George V in 1911.

179

254 The Bell Festival at Middlesmoor, Nidderdale, held annually on 11 June. It began in 1868 when a peal of six bells was given to the church in memory of Simon Horner, a Hull merchant who was a local man. Here the procession is led by the Lofthouse and Middlesmoor Silver Band to be followed by a service in church and a children's tea and fête (1967).

255 Peace celebrations at Austwick after the First World War held on 20 September 1919.

256 Members of the Ancient Order of Foresters at Carlton, Coverdale, on the occasion of their club walk on 9 June 1965. The chief rangers and Robin Hood (a boy) wear traditional green and gold uniforms. Formed in the 1840s for mutual insurance, they now give to charities.

Winter

257 The winter of 1947 at Askrigg, Wensleydale. The moor road was totally blocked and no buses ran for six weeks. This winter, beginning in February, compares with those of 1886 and 1895 for hardship and loss of stock.

· Index ·